Propaganda

Anthony Rhodes

EDITED BY
Victor Margolin

PRODUCED
AND ART DIRECTED BY
Harris Lewine

Volume 1

Chelsea House Publishers
New York   London

Rhodes, Anthony Richard Ewart.
Propaganda: the art of persuasion in WW II.

Filmography: p.
1. World War, 1939–1945—Propaganda.
2. Propaganda—History. I. Title.
D810.P6R48   940.54′88   75-17545

ISBN 0-87754-462-X (vol. 1)
0-87754-461-1 (set)

Design: Seymour Chwast

Chelsea House Publishers
Harold Steinberg, Chairman & Publisher
Susan Lusk, Vice President
A Division of Chelsea House Educational Communications, Inc.
133 Christopher Street, New York 10014

Contents

Volume 1

Foreword by Victor Margolin
vii

CHAPTER ONE
The Propagation of the Reich, 1933–1945
9

CHAPTER TWO
Mussolini's New Rome, 1922–1945
65

CHAPTER THREE
Britain Improvises, 1936–1945
105

CHAPTER FOUR
United States: Isolation and Intervention, 1932–1945
137

Volume 2

CHAPTER FIVE
Rule and Resistance in "The New Order," 1936–1945
177

CHAPTER SIX
The Soviet Union: Propaganda for Peace, 1917–1945
209

CHAPTER SEVEN
The Rise and Fall of Japan, 1931–1945
241

Afterword by Daniel Lerner
283

Essay and Filmography by William Murphy
291

Notes on Color Plates by Victor Margolin
305

Bibliography
308

Index
311

Credits
319

Foreword

Though propaganda has never been a substitute for military strength, extensive resources, or skillful negotiation, it has often played an important role in wartime strategy. No one can deny the impact of German propaganda in softening up the French in 1940, nor the part played by Allied propaganda in preparing the German people for surrender after Normandy.

The term "propaganda" in this book covers a multiplicity of uses—from the posters, films, and comic strips which exposed the home front to images of the enemy, to the "psychological warfare" intended to directly influence the action of enemy troops and civilians. In its broadest sense, World War II propaganda was just about anything which affected or confirmed the feelings and behavior of all involved, both toward their own country's efforts and those of their enemies.

Within this broad definition, visual material was selected from public archives and private collections in the United States and Europe. The editor and the author wish to thank the many individuals and institutions who shared their knowledge and provided material from their collections. Washington D.C.: Michael Hardgrove and Jay Robbins of WETA/Channel 26, who made available a valuable collection of photographs; Dr. Edgar Breitenbach, former chief of the Prints and Photographs Division at the Library of Congress, Alan Fern, who presently holds that position, and the division's staff—Milt Kaplan, Elena Millie, Jerry Kerns, and Leroy Bellamy; Mrs. Seely, U.S. Army Photographic Agency; Mayfield Bray, National Archives; Charles McDonald and Joseph Ewing, U.S. Army Office of Military History. New York: Donald Richie and Mary Corliss, Museum of Modern Art Film Library; New York Public Library Theater Collection; Culver Pictures Corp.; Richard Merkin; Les Zeiger; David Stewart Hull; Maurice Horn; Edward R. Tannenbaum; Herb Friedman. Palo Alto: Dr. Franz Lassner and his staff at the Hoover Institution on War, Peace, and Revolution. San Francisco: Bill Blackbeard, director of the San Francisco Academy of Comic Art. London: Joseph Darracott, Barry Kitts, Mike Moody, Jeff Pavey, and Clive Coultass at the Imperial War Museum; Robson Lowe Ltd.; Victoria and Albert Museum; Reginald Aukland; Roger Bell; the Wiener Library. Paris: Mlle. Cécile Coutin, curator of the Musée des Deux Guerres Mondiales; Mme. Migliorini, Bibliothèque de Documentation Internationale Contemporaine, Nanterre; Michel Girard. Brussels: J. R. Leconte and M. Lorette, Musée Royal de l'Armée et d'Histoire Militaire. Amsterdam: Dr. Louis de Jong, director, and Jacob Zwann, archivist, Rijksinstituut voor Oorlogsdocumentatie. Koblenz: Mr. Haupt, Mr. Postupa, and Frau Loenartz, of the Bundesarchiv. Others who helped were Milton Cohen; Philip V. Cannistraro; Peter Robbs, hon. general secretary of the Psywar Society; and James Goodrich of the Missouri State Historical Society. Photographers included Simon Cherpitel, San Francisco; Teddy Schwartz, London; Mr. Bessam, Amsterdam; and Carmelo Catania, Rome.

Also to be thanked are the excellent production team of Harris Lewine, art director, and Seymour Chwast, designer, as well as David Sachs, copyeditor. Andy Norman and Harold Steinberg of Chelsea House showed great patience during the lengthy period necessary to prepare this book.

Victor Margolin

CHAPTER ONE

THE PROPAGATION OF THE REICH
1933-1945

Nothing is easier than leading the people
on a leash. I just hold up a dazzling
campaign poster and they jump through it.
JOSEPH GOEBBELS

When on February 28, 1933, the Reichstag building in Berlin was set on fire, Chancellor Adolf Hitler obtained an emergency decree from President Paul von Hindenburg placing restrictions on personal liberty, including freedom of the press. Thirteen days later, on March 13, the Ministry for Popular Enlightenment and Propaganda was founded under the direction of Dr. Josef Goebbels, to control the press as well as all other means of expression—radio, film, art, and literature. It is most appropriate that propaganda in Nazi Germany should have been considered worthy of an entire government department. No "Ministry for Popular Enlightenment and Propaganda" had ever existed before, in Germany or in any other country. It was a sign of the age of the Common Man, of the hitherto apolitical and uneducated masses now awakening, and in whose manipulation, as the Nazis (and to a lesser extent the Soviets) were first to become aware, lay the secret of political success. Half a decade before they achieved that success, the Nazis were already skillfully using all the new 20th-century media—press, radio, film, and posters—to control, direct, and coordinate the masses. At the height of its power during the Second World War, the Propaganda Ministry was issuing daily directives to the editors of newspapers all over Germany about what to print, in such detail that the papers were virtually written for the editors.

Political propaganda had been used before in the 20th century, by the British in the First World War, but on a limited scale. It was left to Nazi Germany to employ it on such a scale, and with such effect, that by 1939 the German masses seemed completely indoctrinated. To the very end, most of them still believed that Adolf Hitler was a disinterested ruler, even a messiah, concerned above all with their welfare and, ultimately, that of the human race.

How did he acquire this spurious reputation? It is not enough to say that the Germans have always been responsive to patriotic slogans—"The call of duty," "The honor of the race," "The nobility of a soldier's death." There were a number of other factors: Hitler's own almost superhuman energy, his ruthlessness in crushing opposition, his craftiness in "dividing and ruling," and his manipulation of the armed forces. Hitler's use of propaganda, if not necessarily his most effective weapon (compared, say, to military victories), was certainly his most sinister, for it aimed at, and under Goebbels' masterly direction succeeded in, persuading the Germans that the Nazi system would restore their country's greatness.

Hitler had first become aware of propaganda and its uses before the First World War. In his early writings, he referred to the Austrian Marxists in Vienna, "who knew how to flatter the masses." During the war he saw the effect of British propaganda on the soldiers of the Central Powers; he later read Lord Northcliffe's words, "The bombardment of the German mind was almost as important as the bombardment by cannon." Northcliffe's aim was "to produce by propaganda a state of mind in the German army favorable to surrender—to enlighten it about

(Top) A woodcut of a Teutonic warrior from the magazine Die Kunst im Dritten Reich *(Art in the Third Reich). Nazi artists were conservative and used imagery from the past to promote support for the party. (Middle) The indoctrination of young Nazis began at an early age. (Bottom, left) A drawing by Sepp'a (Josef Plank). (Bottom, right) A ring which could also be used as a weapon.*

Sieg oder Unsieg ruht in Gottes Hand/Der Ehre sind wir selber Herr und König!

Two posters from the 1932 German election. Though Hitler, the Nazi candidate, ran on a platform of economic recovery and resurgent nationalism, he was unable to defeat the 84 year old Field Marshall Hindenburg, supported by a coalition of Socialists, Centrists, and liberals. (Top) "German women, think of your children. Vote Hitler." (Bottom) "Our last hope, Hitler," a poster by Mjölnir (Hans Schweitzer).

the hopelessness of its military situation."

Of this Hitler wrote, "What we failed to do in propaganda was done by the enemy with great skill and ingenious deliberation." It is significant that Hitler's first appearance on the political scene was in the role of military propagandist at the end of the war. The officers of the 1st Bavarian Rifle Regiment, in which he was serving, recognized in the voluble corporal a committed nationalist whose oratory might counter the revolutionary Marxism now making headway among the demoralized troops. They made him "regimental political education officer." He was remarkably successful.

A few years later, when he was writing *Mein Kampf (My Struggle)*, he devoted two chapters to the study and practice of propaganda. Although he said that in the future the man who controlled the masses would control the state, he made no attempt to hide his contempt for the masses. "The psyche of the masses," he wrote, "is not receptive to anything that is weak. They are like a woman, whose psychic state is determined less by abstract reason than by an emotional longing for a strong force which will complement her nature. Likewise, the masses love a commander, and despise a petitioner."

To his friend Rauschnigg he said, "Haven't you ever seen a crowd collecting to watch a street brawl? Brutality and physical strength is what they respect. The man in the street respects nothing more than strength and ruthlessness—women too for that matter. The masses need something that will give them a thrill of horror." For the next fifteen years, Hitler was to give them just that, in ever increasing measure.

He started from the premise that propaganda must be addressed to the emotions and not to the intelligence; and it must concentrate on a few simple themes, presented in black and white. "Propaganda," he wrote, "consists in attracting the crowd, and not in educating those who are already educated." He had no use for the intelligentsia or the upper classes.

He first put his theories into practice in 1925, in the Nazi party newspaper, the *Völkischer Beobachter (People's Observer)*. It contained none of the long, rambling articles and academic discussions which characterized the liberal bourgeois, socialist, and communist presses, but instead short, sharp hyperboles on "patriotic" themes—The Infamy of Versailles, the Nobility of the Teutons, The Weakness of Weimar, The Virus of Jewry, The Evil of Bolshevism, and the ringing slogan *"Ein Volk, Ein Reich, Ein Führer"* (one people, one nation, one leader).

This paper, and others which the Party subsequently acquired (such as the anti-Semitic *Der Stürmer*), were all characterized by Hitler's statement about the masses' admiration of violence. Their propaganda was vicious and gruesome, with lurid photographs of the atrocities, sexual and physical, alleged to have been committed by Jews and communists on unsuspecting German women.

As leader of the Party, Hitler was too busy to devote much time to propaganda, important though he recognized it to be. It required a full-time expert. In Josef Goebbels he found his man.

Goebbels was to become one of history's greatest political propagandists. A Rhinelander of humble origins, he had obtained a number of scholarships to universities and became a doctor of philosophy. Hitler met him in 1926 and, quickly appreciating his oratorical power of persuasion, made him head of the party propaganda department. It is probable that Goebbels—a cynic in most matters—genuinely admired, even hero-worshipped, Hitler. Goebbels and many like him had suffered from the political and economic chaos in Germany in the early 1920s; in Hitler he saw the savior of his country from both chaos and communism. He immediately set about creating the Führer legend which was to carry Hitler and his Party to power, and to make Hitler revered throughout Germany.

Goebbels had studied the methods employed by the Fascists in Italy to create the heroic image of Mussolini; and he applied them a fortiori to Hitler. He realized that to impress the masses, the modern dictator must be at once a superman and a man of the people, remote yet accessible, wise yet simple, lonely on his Olympian height, yet ready to mix with the crowd. This is seen in two articles which Goebbels wrote in his paper *Der Angriff* (*The Attack*)—"Adolf Hitler, Statesman," and "Adolf Hitler, Human Being." In the first, he showed the Führer as infallible in his political judgments, which were beyond human acumen; yet he was, as the second article showed, surprisingly human and kind. "The simplest people," Goebbels wrote, "approach him with confidence, because they feel he is their friend and protector."

Hitler was, he argued, really an artist, an architect and painter, who had forsaken his muse to help the German people in their darkest hour. When he had completed his political work, he would return to his calling. For Germany's sake he had learned to negotiate with all the statesmen of Europe, in polished dialogue and with a masterly command of diplomacy, for days on end, sometimes in fifteen-hour sessions.

In his many public speeches and articles in *Der Angriff* before the Party attained power, Goebbels was also careful to depict the Führer as a man of the people, who had shared their plight and knew their problems. He described, for instance, how Hitler once visited his native land at Oberammergau and mingled with the Austrian crowd, speaking to one or two of them. So moved were they by his kind and understanding words that they were unable to answer because "their tears choked them." Goebbels described how the goodness of the man shone out in his face: "His eyes are bright with unimpaired radiance, his high forehead is noble and bold. Only his hair reveals a light silver touch, the sign of countless days of work and worry and nights in which he is awake and lonely. Never does one word of falsehood or baseness pass his lips."

Goebbels occasionally introduced a religious note about this paragon of virtues. Of a speech Hitler made in Cologne he wrote, "One had the feeling as if all Germany had been transformed into one vast church embracing all classes and creeds, in which its spokesman appeared before the high altar of the Almighty to

The Illustrierter Beobachter *was a popular tabloid newspaper filled with photographs of meetings, demonstrations, and processions. Reporting was confined almost exclusively to glorifying the Nazi movement. Articles on all topics were heavily slanted. (Top) "They fought and bled for Germany's freedom," 1942. (Bottom) "Russia arms! . . . and Germany?," 1933.*

Sie kämpften und bluteten für Deutschlands Freiheit

Russland rüstet!
. . . und Deutschland?

Sowjetrussische Schulkinder beim Waffenunterricht

Posters, photomontages, and magazine
covers by John Heartfield, a Communist
designer who attacked the Nazis until
the party was banned after Hitler
became Chancellor. (Bottom, left)
"6 million Nazi voters; fodder for a
huge mouth." (Top, right) Stamps for a
1932 peace congress. (Bottom, right) A
play on the proverb, "Lies have short
legs." Opposite page. (Top row, left)
"Adolf—the superman; swallows gold
and talks nonsense." (Top row, middle)
"Have no fear; he's a vegetarian."
(Top row, right) Hitler as a Prussian
officer. (Middle row, left) "Göring the
hangman." (Middle row, middle)
"The bishop of the Reich inspects the
Christian ranks." (Middle row, right)
"The cross wasn't heavy enough."
(Bottom row, left) "Blood and Iron,
the old election slogan in the new
Reich." (Bottom row, middle) "New
chair in the German universities."
(Bottom row, right) A Christmas tree
in the shape of a swastika.

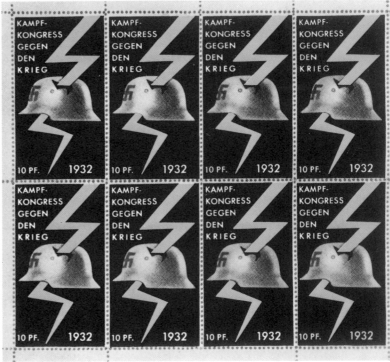

6 Millionen Naziwähler: Futter für ein großes Maul

„Und den Fisch hab ich gewählt!"

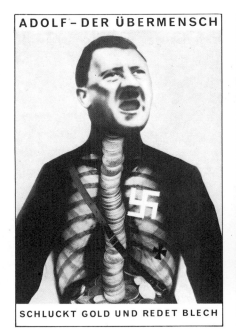

ADOLF – DER ÜBERMENSCH

SCHLUCKT GOLD UND REDET BLECH

NUR KEINE ANGST — ER IST VEGETARIER

S.M. ADOLF

Ich
führe Euch herrlichen Pleiten entgegen!

GÖRING, DER HENKER

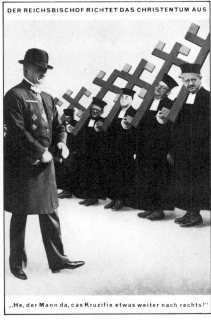

DER REICHSBISCHOF RICHTET DAS CHRISTENTUM AUS

„He, der Mann da, das Kruzifix etwas weiter nach rechts!"

ZUR GRÜNDUNG DER STAATSKIRCHE

Das Kreuz war noch nicht schwer genug

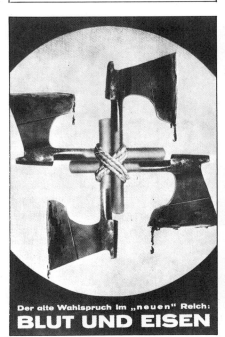

Der alte Wahlspruch im „neuen" Reich:
BLUT UND EISEN

Neuer Lehrstuhl an den deutschen Universitäten

Ein Professor Witlawopsky vor der Universität Heidelberg hat festgestellt, daß das menschliche Hühnerauge, allerdings nur das germanische, befähigt ist, in die Zukunft zu schauen. Hitler hat sogleich nach Bekanntwerden der Entdeckung des genialen Forschers die Überführung von 1200 Hühneraugen-Operateuren ins Konzentrationslager angeordnet.
Originalaufnahme aus dem teutonischen Busch von J. H.

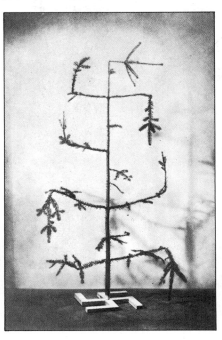

(Below) "The Field Marshall and the Corporal," a 1933 poster which showed Hitler and Hindenburg as partners in shaping Germany's future. In March 1933, the Nazis pushed through legislation enabling Hitler to rule unsupervised. (Opposite page, top and middle, left) Medals commemorating the Nuremberg rallies in 1935 and 1936. (Bottom, left) National Socialist Party songbook. (Top, right) Burial ceremony for Horst Wessel, an S.A. tough who was killed by the Communists in 1930 and martyred by Goebbels. A song he wrote, the Horst Wessel Lied became the official song of the Nazi party and the second national anthem after Deutschland über Alles. *(Middle, right) Nazi troops hold a banner at a Party Day rally in Nuremberg. (Bottom, right) Hitler was a supreme orator who could play on the emotions of a crowd. He was at his best before a mass audience and, unlike Roosevelt, was ineffective in a broadcast studio.*

render an account of his achievements, and to implore His mercy and protection for the uncertain future. In Cologne that morning, we saw hard and strong men who had overcome many a danger burst into tears at the closing words of the Führer. This was religion in the most mysterious and deepest sense of the word."

Goebbels even went so far on one occasion as to introduce a mother image of this essentially masculine man. "And so, the whole nation loves him because it feels safe in his hands, like a child in the arms of its mother."

How did Goebbels explain the Führer's role in the events of June 30, 1934, "The Night of the Long Knives"? On that occasion, Hitler ordered, and personally supervised, the butchery of some 150 of his former comrades, whom he suspected of plotting to take over the army. The morning after the slaughter, Goebbels printed a photograph of the Führer in which he stressed "the tragic loneliness in his face"; for the Führer had become "another Siegfried who has been forced to shed blood so that Germany might live." His face reflected "grief and sorrow over the deaths of his Old Comrades who had been misled."

Had not the Führer himself said that all his actions were dictated by a higher power? "I go," he said, "with the assurance of a sleepwalker in the path which providence dictates." He was the rock in the ocean of peoples' lives, as well as Atlas bearing on his shoulders the cares of Germany and the whole world, which he alone could save from the Jews and communists.

Another photograph of the Führer which Goebbels continually reproduced was of Hitler with the universally loved but moribund President von Hindenburg. "The Führer's face," wrote Goebbels, "here reflects grief and sadness over the merciless death about to take away his fatherly friend." (In fact, far from being a "fatherly friend," Hindenburg could not bear the sight of Hitler, whom he always referred to as "the Bohemian corporal." Hitler, for his part, was longing for Hindenburg to die, so that he could take over his job.)

For his creation of the Führer legend, Goebbels made great use of the mass demonstrations which became a regular feature of Nazi Germany after Hitler's assumption of power. Emotional manipulation, he found, was most effective at these mammoth gatherings, when both participants and onlookers became part of the Führer intoxication, when each single individual underwent, in his words, "a kind of metamorphosis from a little worm into part of a big dragon." These demonstrations generally took place at night, after 8 P.M., when people's resistance was at its lowest ebb, and their minds most open to persuasion. At the annual rally in Nuremberg, the Nazis' holy city, half a million people on the tribunes watched 200,000 banner-carrying uniformed men belonging to a plethora of Nazi organizations march past the Führer, who stood on a dais for all to see.

Albert Speer, Hitler's favorite architect, was the "chief decorator" of the rallies. He devised the idea of placing 130 anti-aircraft searchlights around the rally field at intervals of forty feet. He called the ring of vertical beams a "cathedral of light."

(*Top and bottom*) *Leni Riefenstahl,*
whose film of the 1934 Nuremberg
rally, Triumph of the Will, *became a*
classic of film propaganda. Heavy-
handed in its symbolism and tedious in
its endless shots of marching troops,
Triumph of the Will *was*
nevertheless used to create
the impression of Nazi strength and
discipline. Though the film appears to
be a documentary, the rally was as
carefully staged for the camera's sake
as a Cecil B. DeMille epic.

At the 1936 rally, after a torchlight procession 150 searchlights converged in a vast cupola in the sky above the multitude. Speer also designed a huge eagle over 100 feet in wingspread to crown the stands. Fanfares sounded and bands played the Führer's favorite march, the *Badenweiler*, as erect, grim-faced, jackbooted, he trod the podium. His personal standard was unfurled and suddenly, at a shrill command, 30,000 flags dipped in salute. The entire ceremony centered around the Führer's podium, where the Man of Destiny stood alone with upraised arm. He then addressed the multitude over the loudspeaker network in a harangue which sometimes lasted an hour, and which rose at the end to a crescendo of hysteria. It dealt with the old hackneyed patriotic themes—the heroic struggle of the Party to restore Germany's greatness, the pollution of the Jews, the beastliness of the Bolsheviks, the decadence of the democracies. When he had finished, the flags were dipped again and half a million people sang the national anthem, *Deutschland über Alles*, and Goebbel's Party hymn, the *Horst Wessel Lied*. In the silence that then fell, he shrieked, "Hail, my men!", and the multitude bayed back, "Hail my Führer!" (The use of *my* instead of *our* gave each individual the feeling that it was *his* Führer, to whom he belonged.)

The Führer then consecrated the new Party colors by touching them with one hand, while the other grasped the cloth of the bullet-riddled *Blutfahne*, the flag drenched in the gore of the Nazi martyrs who had carried it to their death in the abortive putsch of 1923. The whole parade finished in a welter of fanfares, drum beats, flaring pylons, massed choruses, and banner-waving marching columns passing before the Führer, beneath triumphal arches adorned with stylized eagles clutching wreathed swastikas.

Hitler had likened these emotional masses to a woman, and it was the women of Germany who were most fanatical and hysterical on these occasions. He was always receiving letters from female admirers imploring him to father their children. It was even said that mothers-to-be in labor often called out his name to ease the pain.

By the outbreak of the Second World War, Goebbels' Propaganda Ministry had complete control of the press, radio, theater, cinema, the creative arts, music, writing, art exhibitions. When every contemporary book people read, every newspaper, every film they see, every broadcast they hear for years on end is permeated with the same spirit, the same propaganda, they are no longer able to relate what they see and hear to alternative reports; they lose their judgment. By 1939 no one thought it odd, let alone funny, that a Nazi sports leader proclaimed to the cycling clubs of Germany, "The Führer demands the unity of the whole German cycling movement"; or that bowlers were informed that their sport now enjoyed its high position in the public esteem entirely due to the Führer.

Goebbels openly admitted that propaganda had little to do with the truth. "Historical truth," he said at a mass meeting in Berlin, "may be discovered by a professor of history. *We* however are serving historical necessity. It is not its task, any more than it is the task of art, to be objectively true." The sole aim of propaganda, he said, was success. Here he was claiming for propaganda what Machiavelli had proclaimed 500 years before as the sole aim of statesmanship.

All the same, Goebbels was careful not to tell whole lies; he was a master at distorting the truth. In the words of Schwerin von Krosig, "He hid the nucleus of truth with all the veils of interpretation. He always had a channel of escape when anyone questioned the truth of his statement."

The cinema was Goebbel's special foster child. He not only had a personal weakness for female screen idols (a number of whom became his mistresses), but he was quick to realize that this new art form could reach a far wider audience than books or theater. The notion of thousands of adult men and women all cooped up in the dark, staring at the same image on the silver screen appealed to his sense of uniformity. Also, the film with its well-worn cliches—suspense, adventure, love, crime, murder—could be addressed to the lowest common denominator of the human intellect. Thanks to governmental stimulus, cinema attendance quadrupled in the ten-year period from 1933 to 1942.

Because the Nazis considered the cinema such a powerful medium, its personnel—actors, directors, electricians, cameramen, etc.—were immediately made to take the oath of loyalty to the Führer. As early as May 1, 1934, five thousand employees of the UFA studios took it, without apparent demur. The old Motion Picture Law of 1920 was replaced by the Reich Motion Picture Law, which enacted that the subject of every proposed film must be "handed in before the making of the film to the Reich Film Drama Advisor in outline and scenario form for examination." Paragraph 2, Section 5 stated that the censor's aim must be "to hinder such subject matter as runs counter to the spirit of the times."

Goebbels took a personal interest in all the films made during the Third Reich, and he often intervened personally to make a change or an addition. His known addiction to the cinema sometimes caused unexpected, even embarassing situations. Once, he had seen a preview of a film about hospital life—the usual love story of doctors and nurses—and he was on his way to another appointment. In his hurry, he said in passing to his adjutant, "Now, we've had enough of these *Arztefilms* (doctor films) to last us a long time. Tell them—no more!" But the adjutant thought he said "*Ernstefilms*" (serious films). He dutifully transmitted the instructions to the screen writers, with the result that for months after the Propaganda Ministry was flooded with quantities of light comedies—and this at a time (1943) when the Nazi leaders wanted people to be fortified by serious and heroic films, of the Frederick the Great type.

The best-known films of the Nazi period are Leni Riefenstahl's *Triumph of the Will*, about the 1934 Nuremberg Rally, in the documentary form she perfected, and her *Olympia*, another documentary about the 1936 Olympic Games in Berlin. Both are Nazi propaganda, but of a relatively subtle kind. The former

(Top) A scene from Leni Riefenstahl's Triumph of the Will. *The three huge banners behind the podium were designed by Albert Speer, Hitler's chief architect. Riefenstahl's second full-length propaganda film was* Olympia, *the subject of which was the 1936 Olympic games in Berlin. (Below) A Dutch poster protesting the 1936 Olympics.*

de olympiade onder dictatuur
tentoonstelling:
sport, kunst, wetenschap, documenten

amsterdam
augustus
1936
gebouw
de geelvinck
singel 530

(Top) A page from a Nazi textbook. (Bottom) A scene from Eduard von Borsody's film, The Trial of Binnie Casilla *(1939), a mockery of American press and court procedures. A man is tried for kidnapping his own daughter from her foster parents. The child becomes a film star and the foster parents, not wishing to lose her income, regularly inject her with a serum to prevent her growth. The father's German origin raises antipathy in court but he finally wins the case.*

Mein Führer!

(Das Kind spricht:)

Ich kenne dich wohl und habe dich lieb
              wie Vater und Mutter.
Ich will dir immer gehorsam sein
              wie Vater und Mutter.
Und wenn ich groß bin, helfe ich dir
              wie Vater und Mutter,
Und freuen sollst du dich an mir
              wie Vater und Mutter!

opens on the heavens with magnificent shots of cloud formations behind which the threatening sound of Hitler's bombers can be heard. The Führer is seen alighting from an airplane, and then the whole Nuremberg Rally is filmed. With her technical skill, Riefenstahl was able to present the Party and its leaders in a heroic light for Germans, and a respectable one for foreigners. The film also fostered the feeling of the participation of the masses in the ceremony. "The preparations for the rally" wrote Riefenstahl, "were made in concert with the preparations for the camera work." That is, the rally was planned not only as a spectacle, but as spectacular film propaganda. The arenas and approaches for the Olympic Games were designed and constructed in the same way, as much for Riefenstahl's army of cameramen as for the athletes.

The Olympic Games proved an ideal vehicle for Nazi propaganda to foreign countries. At the previous games, in Amsterdam in 1928 and Los Angeles in 1932, no arrangements had been made for simultaneous broadcasting of the events as they took place. At Berlin in 1936, during the sixteen days of the games, 2,500 reports were broadcast in twenty-eight languages by German and foreign reporters. Afterwards, the foreign press and radio correspondents sent congratulatory telegrams to Goebbels on this admirable organization. Goebbels personally supervised the propaganda arrangements and produced an image of a smiling, jovial people filled with vitality. The result was that many of the foreign dignitaries, suitably wined and dined, came away deeply impressed by the New Germany. For the benefit of these visitors, the Nazis soft-pedaled much of their propaganda. All anti-Semitic regulations, such as "Jews not admitted," were removed from hotels and restaurants. Julius Streicher's anti-Semitic *Der Stürmer* could not be bought on the streets, and other aggressive propaganda measures were suspended or abated. The only discordant note—from the Nazi point of view —was the success of the black American sprinter, Jesse Owens, who received more international attention than any other athlete. But Leni Riefenstahl was careful not to show Hitler petulantly leaving the stadium when Owens ran.

Jüd Süss (*Jew Süss*) was a different form of propaganda, a nauseating anti-Semitic film. Set in the Middle Ages, it depicts a repulsive, crooked-nosed Jew who threatens a German maiden: if she does not let him ravish her, he will have her fiancé broken on the wheel. After the rape the heroine, like a good German, commits suicide. The hanging of the Jew at the end was described by a German critic as a "joyous crescendo." The actress in this film was one of the Nazi screen favorites, Kristina Söderbaum, a snub-nosed Nordic blond who was often cast in roles of this kind. In another film, from Billinger's novel *Gigant*, she plays a Sudeten German peasant's daughter who becomes bewitched by the lure of a big city and forsakes her father's hearth for Prague. She pays for worshipping this false (Czech) idol by first being made pregnant and then deserted by her Czech seducer. She returns home, where her old father is so ashamed of her behavior that he commits suicide. In the film version however, the ending is different, because the Propaganda Ministry insisted that the disgraced daughter, not the guiltless father, should suffer for the racial pollution. In her films, Kristina Söderbaum generally committed suicide by drowning. This became such a convention that the end always showed her—whether she had suffered rape, seduction, or desertion—floating Ophelia-like on the water. For this she became popularly known as the *Reichswasserleiche* (the national floating corpse).

Another way in which the Propaganda Ministry interfered was in the censorship of foreign films. It banned the French film *Nana*, based on Zola's novel, because of a scene between a soldier and a prostitute. Since the army is the foundation of the state, ran the argument, to depict a soldier cohabitating with a prostitute undermines the state's authority.

One of the most important uses of the cinema was for the indoctrination of the young. In April 1934, the first "Film Hour for the Young" was opened in Cologne. Two months later Goebbels' film administrator, Dr. Rust, ordered the showing of "politically valuable films" in all schools throughout the Reich. In his directive he said, "To disseminate our National Socialist ideology we know of no better medium than the film—above all for the youngest of our citizens, the schoolchildren. The National Socialist state deliberately makes the film the transmitter of its ideology."

Within two years Rust had equipped 70,000 schools with motion picture projectors. The cinema attendance in schools increased from 650,000 children in 1934 to 3 million in 1939. Two hundred and twenty-seven films were produced for schools. They dealt with "the great problems of our epoch," which were nothing less than the preparations, mental and emotional, for war.

The theme of nearly all these school films was *Wehrerziehung* (military education), and their protagonist was the UFA film director, Karl Ritter, a fanatical Nazi. His films glorified death in battle; films like *A Pass in Promise* in which a young composer prefers to die in November 1918 fighting for an already conquered Germany, rather than live on for the première of his symphony. As Ritter himself said, "My films all deal with the unimportance of the individual. . . . all that is personal is as nothing compared with the Cause." His film *Traitors and Patriots*, which romanticized fifth column activities in foreign countries, was shown to some 6 million schoolboys.

The effect of these films was inordinate. Many of the Hitler Youth who had been herded by the thousands into the cinemas to see them were taken prisoner during the war. Under Allied interrogation, they revealed the influence these films had had on them. Arrogant in victory, cold and unperturbed in defeat, they openly confessed that they were, as individuals, utterly unimportant, and that in war their sole function was to be instruments.

Nazi society was completely male dominated, and some of these films, such as *Hitlerjunge Quex*, have overtones of homosexuality. Writers like Ernst Jünger had advocated the substitution of male comradeship for love. The Nazis had no particular

Scenes from three films on Nazi youth. (Top) A film on the Hitlerjugend *(Hitler Youth Movement). (Middle) Hans Steinhoff's* Hitlerjunge Quex, *one of several feature films on party themes made in 1933. (Bottom) S.A. Mann Brandt (1933), directed by Franz Seitz. After these initial party films, Goebbels encouraged features that were more entertaining or less overtly propagandistic.*

Nazi propagandists had enough faith in Hitler's charisma to print this 1932 election poster of his disembodied head floating on a black background. Erwin Schockel wrote of this poster in Das Politische Plakat (1938), "Peace, strength, and goodness radiate from Hitler's face and are communicated to the viewer. The effect on men with uncorrupted souls must be good." The heavy square lettering reflects the ponderous Nazi taste in graphic design. (Opposite, full page) Hitler in the pose of a Renaissance prince. The slogan on the poster, One people, one nation, one leader, was often used in the Reich. (Opposite, inset) The single word Ja (Yes) combined with the forceful image of Hitler expresses confidence in his leadership.

moral objection to homosexuality as a physical act. Why then was homosexuality so savagely punished in the Third Reich? Because, quite simply, it was sabotage—sabotage of the nation's future manpower.

A feature peculiar to 20th-century dictatorships is their concern with reaching the juvenile mind. Youth is to be courted by the state, trained, educated, organized, and finally marshaled. Already in the Weimar period the Nazis had been successfully wooing the youth of Germany, who, during the 1920s, had been much neglected by the Weimar government; they had become aimless, skeptical and pseudoromantic, waiting for something to fill the void and give them what they wanted—a sense of importance and some emotional involvement.

Goebbels' propagandists found the youth an easy prey. With unlimited appeal to the emotions and ruthless exploitation of their readiness to believe and follow, the Nazis had won the German youth several years before they assumed power. During these years the principal attraction for the young people was the "new comradeship of the Hitler Youth"—the Hitler parade of uniforms, in marked contrast to the drabness of everyday life in the Weimar Republic.

Until as late as 1936 a number of youth organizations, such as the Catholic Youth and the Boy Scouts, existed in Germany alongside the Hitler Youth. In that year Baldur von Schirach, leader of the Hitler Youth, gave an order that all these organizations were henceforth forbidden to take part in any form of organized sport. Now, if a young man belonged to the Catholic Youth or any other of the organizations apart from the Hitler Youth, all forms of organized sport—athletics, hiking, skiing, gymnastics, even camping—were denied him. In addition, Schirach forbade all members of youth movements (apart from the Hitler Youth) to wear uniforms, together with badges, shoulder straps, lanyards, etc. They were also forbidden to march in formation, have their own bands, carry flags, banners, and pennants. These measures reveal the Nazis' understanding of the juvenile mind.

The *Bund deutscher Mädchen* (German Girls' League) was the female counterpart of the Hitler Youth. It too had a monopoly of all sport for girls. They attended Youth Hostel weekends, where they learned to run 60 meters in 12 seconds, swim 100 meters, throw a ball over a distance of 20 meters. Like the boys, they had to learn all the facts about the Führer and his "days of struggle," as well as the names of Hitler Youth "martyrs." The girls wore white blouses, almost ankle-length skirts, and sturdy shoes.

Concurrently with the cinema as a means of visual propaganda appeared the poster. This apparently simple form of advertisement played a greater part in the Nazis' rise to power than is generally realized. Goebbels' propagandists knew that visual impressions are extremely strong, that people may forget a newspaper article, but not a picture—if they see it often and its message is obvious. In this respect the poster had certain advan-

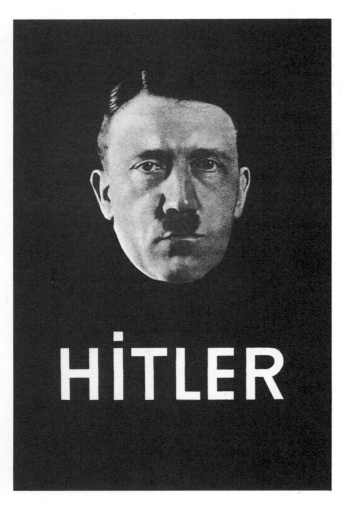

HİTLER

Ja!

Ein Volk, ein Reich, ein Führer!

Two versions of a poster by Mjölnir (Hans Schweitzer) who perfected the image of the iron-jawed Storm Trooper. (Top) "The organized will of the nation," the later version of Mjölnir's 1932 election poster. (Bottom) The earlier cruder version of the same poster from the late 1920s. Nazi troopers of this period were shown as tough revolutionaries. Mjölnir was the graphic artist most closely associated with the Nazi party.

tages over the other forms of propaganda. A pamphlet or a newspaper could be thrown away, unread; the radio turned off; political meetings not attended; likewise the cinema. But everyone at some time or other walked in the streets. The poster could not be avoided. It was one thing to hear about Hitler's strength of character, sincerity, honesty, simplicity, etc.; it was quite another to see these qualities glaring down from a huge head-and-shoulders portrait, ten times life-size. If the passerby averted his eyes, he ran into Hitler again around the corner. No inhabited place in Germany was without him, nor "the heroic German male" about whom the Nazis were always boasting. Suddenly in the street on the opposite wall he stood—lantern-jawed, erect, determined, puissant, girding himself to defend Germany from "the Red Terror" or "the Jewish Bacillus."

The master of these political posters, on whom was bestowed the title of "Reich Plenipotentiary for Artistic Formulation," was the artist Mjölnir (Hans Schweitzer). As a Nazi leader once said, "What lengthy speeches failed to do, Mjölnir did in a second through the glowing fanaticism of his powerful art." Mjölnir's poster of the three Storm Troopers' heads is quintessential Nazi propaganda—simple, emotional, powerful. Hitler had said, "by the masses, brutality and physical force are admired." Here they are. These are three Nazi "fighters," one young, the second middle-aged, the third an older man, who have all clearly passed through the fires of combat, in the trenches or the streets, and whose faces have a male strength verging on brutality. Done in 1932, one poster depicts the "Aryan" fighting to bring the Nazi movement to power. The other prominent poster designer of the Third Reich was Ludwig Hohlwein, one of Germany's leading commercial artists. Unlike Mjölnir, he idealized the fair-haired youth so admired by the Nazis.

The same principles of propaganda posters held good for postage stamps. The stamp reaches an even larger public than the poster. Stamps on envelopes referring to the Saar referendum in 1935 brought the subject to the attention of the entire German people. There were Party rally stamps; Hitler's birthday stamps; stamps referring to the return of Eupen and Malmedy to the fatherland; to the union of Germany and Austria. In all German post offices stamped postcards were sold bearing slogans and quotations from Hitler's speeches. There were Hitler Youth stamps and a Hitler stamp souvenir sheet with the slogan, "He who wants to serve a people can think only in heroic terms." That the Nazis appreciated this form of propaganda is seen in their prohibition of the sale of Soviet stamps to collectors in Germany between 1933 and 1939, and between 1941 and 1945.

In the other visual arts, the Nazis were not as successful as they were with the poster; more intellectual forms of art could not be made to serve their purposes as effectively. However, if only for foreign consumption, they had to show some concern for it.

They used pictorial art in two ways: as an illustration of what they called the moral and material decay of their predecessors, the men of Weimar with their "decadent Expressionism," and to propagate their own "Aryan" policies. For the first, many who could not understand modern art could be convinced that it was indeed degenerate and rotten. The Nazis simply selected the least successful works of the Expressionist artists—and their more abstract and extreme experiments—and displayed them all over the country in a series of elaborate exhibitions entitled "Degenerate Art." The exhibits were so displayed as to shock people, hung with the intention of making the artists appear at their worst. The public which came in thousands were told that their money, in taxes, had been spent by the Weimar government on these abominations. They could see for themselves how cynically the Expressionist artists treated such sacred themes as love, "the German woman," heroes, and the fatherland. All had been mocked and reviled. They were told that Jewish dealers had made fortunes out of peddling this "trash."

The "Nazi art" which replaced this was also used as an instrument of propaganda. It is significant that Nazi painting can easily be described in words because the subject matter is more important than the form. For the Nazis, the range of these subjects was limited: peasants with large families, emphasizing the importance of the German soil and fertility; allegories of the Muses, an opportunity to depict nubile nudes of pure Aryan descent; fair-haired, uniformed marching boys with banners and swastika flags; lantern-jawed Storm Troopers in steel helmets, with clenched fists, in action or participating in some national ceremony; and then the Führer himself in heroic pose, sometimes wearing medieval armor in the role of the new St. George slaying the Jewish-Bolshevik dragon. The titles are self-explanatory: *The Last Hand Grenade, The New Youth, The Guardian of the Race, Make Room for the SA, The Pilot, The Day of Potsdam 1933.*

Many of the paintings took the form of murals. The revival of the mural was in fact one of the most important features of Nazi art. The Nazis postulated coordination of all the arts in their public buildings, particularly of architecture and mural decoration. The proportions of mural and fresco paintings suited their grandiloquence, as well as providing work for thousands of artists on vast surfaces. The propaganda value of these huge paintings, which forced themselves on the eye of every visitor to the ministries, Party buildings, public halls, and schools which housed them, was considerable. Even those who never entered the Haus der Deutschen Kunst (House of German Art) in Munich could not escape them, because they were reproduced in newspapers and magazines all over the country. Well-produced art publications were also devoted to Nazi Art. The most elaborate of these, *Die Kunst im Dritten Reich* (*Art in the Third Reich*), was beautifully laid out, with paper and color plates of the highest quality.

It was not the artistic influence of these paintings which mattered, for there was little artistic about them; it was the content. To the impressionable youth of Germany, these pictures reinforced what they were being taught in school—the supremacy of the Teutons, the injustices to which they had been subjected

(Top) A massive relief figure by Arno Brecker, one of the Third Reich's official sculptors. (Bottom) Jacob Epstein with an example of his "degenerate" sculpture. Works by Epstein and other modern artists were displayed at a 1937 exhibition of "degenerate art," which backfired as propaganda by becoming the most popular exhibit ever mounted in the Reich.

*Albert Speer, the chief architect of
the Third Reich, envisioned Berlin
as the capital of a world empire.
The buildings he designed according
to gigantic proportions were "to tower
up like the cathedrals of our past
into the millennia to come." Architecture
as propaganda was intended to
impress people with the power and
solidity of the Reich. (Top, middle,
and bottom) Three sections of Speer's
model of Berlin: the Great Basin,
Tempelhof Airport, and the
German Plaza.*

GROSSES BECKEN - JUNI 1938

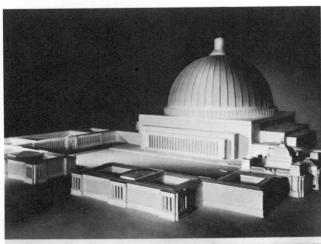

DEUTSCHER PLATZ   JANUAR 1937

since 1919, the romance of war, the superiority of the physical over the intellectual.

Even in the sports grounds where the Germans sought recreation, in the parks and forests around their towns, the new art was prominent, generally in the form of vast statues, representing the vigor of Germany's manhood, with bulging muscles and energetic attitudes. The sculptors Arno Brecker and Josef Thorak were responsible for many of these gargantuan monuments. When on one occasion a visitor to Thorak's studio asked, "Where is the sculptor?" an assistant replied, "Up in the left ear of the horse."

The very streets of the cities were transformed into propaganda. Trees were uprooted and houses pulled down to make room for the great mass demonstrations. The ponderous new buildings in the various cities, particularly in Berlin, Munich, and Nuremberg, with their huge squares and courtyards and rows of neoclassical columns, were conceived as a background for the marching SS. Albert Speer, the great architect of the Third Reich, built Hitler's pompous chancellery in Berlin, a combination of ancient Greece and Prussian classicism, decorated with Nazi symbols. He also planned the reconstruction of the capital on a grand scale, as befitted the metropolis of the Nazi empire.

As the Party owed its success in propaganda more to the spoken than to the printed word, it is understandable that the other 20th-century discovery of which Goebbels made good use was the radio. He once said that radio would do for the 20th century what newspapers had done for the 19th. He regarded it, he said, "as an important means toward the uniformity of the German people—in north and south, east and west, of Catholic and Protestant, or bourgeois, workers, and peasants." (Significantly he made no reference to the upper classes whom he, like Hitler, regarded as of no importance.) "With this instrument," he told the heads of his radio stations, "you can make public opinion." Hitler, too, was well aware of this; in his first year as chancellor he made over fifty major broadcasts. These were speeches at meetings and rallies rather than studio broadcasts. Hitler attempted one studio broadcast, but felt uncomfortable without the presence of a visible audience.

Before 1933, the big German cities all had their radio stations emitting their own programs. In contrast to this decentralization, Goebbels concentrated the control of all broadcasting in Berlin, under his Propaganda Ministry, which was, significantly, sometimes referred to as the *Befehlszentrale*, the center for issuing orders.

To increase the number of listeners, the Nazis put on the market one of the cheapest wireless sets in Europe. It was heavily subsidized so that it cost no more than a worker's weekly salary; it was appropriately known as the VE (*Volksempfänger*, peoples' radio). The aim was to install a set in every home in Germany. As that goal would not be reached for some time, communal listening was also encouraged, in the factories, offices, restaurants, cafes, even at street corners. When a speech by a Nazi leader or an important announcement was to be made, factories and offices had to stop work so that everyone could listen. In 10,000 restaurants throughout the Reich, when the announcement *"Der Führer spricht"* was made over the radio, diners felt embarrassed to go on masticating while the harsh and familiar sounds reverberated around the room.

Another technique used was the "radio warden" for each block of houses or apartment buildings. This Party member would encourage his neighbors who did not own a radio to buy one (sometimes he would lend them the money to do so); otherwise, to listen to important speeches in his or a friend's home. He sent in regular reports on their reactions to the broadcasts. Thus, when a program on the importance of having large families was greeted by a listener with the jocular "Not for me! Grandpa had diabetes," he was reported and taken severely to task. The radio warden became of special importance during the war when he reported those listening to foreign broadcasts.

Listeners soon learned to recognize the signature tunes associated with the various Party leaders. Hitler's imminent arrival at any gathering was invariably preceded by his favorite march, the *Badenweiler*. Goebbels' annual eulogy on the Führer's birthday was always preceded by Wagner's *Meistersinger* Overture, and Hitler's speech on Heroes Day by the second movement of Beethoven's *Eroica* Symphony.

Between 1933 and 1939 the number of private radio sets in Germany quadrupled. The radio was also important for influencing foreign opinion. Other nations could prohibit the import of Nazi written propaganda, but it was much harder to interfere with a radio broadcast. The radio played a great part in both the Saar plebiscite and the Anschluss (union) with Austria.

The rich industrial area of the Saar valley had been occupied by France since the end of the First World War; the region's status was to be decided by a plebiscite in 1935. The Nazi propaganda campaign for the Saar plebiscite was begun over a year earlier. In January 1934, Goebbels set up an office for radio transmission to the Saar. Every Wednesday a series, "The Saar —the Way to Understanding is Clear" was broadcast. Between January 1934 and April 1935, some 4,000 *Volksempfänger* radio sets were distributed in the Saarland. The French made only a last-minute attempt to influence the Saarlanders by broadcasting. Undoubtedly the Saar plebiscite would have returned the territory to Germany, but not with the large majority—over 90 percent—which Goebbels' radio campaign insured.

In planning the enforced Anschluss with Austria, the big Nazi transmitter in Munich played an important part. The Austrian transmitters were not as powerful, and for three or four years before the Anschluss, the Austrian people were bombarded aurally each night with propaganda about the great German Führer, about what he had done for Germany—and what, if invited, he would do for Austria. It is significant, too, that at the time of the abortive 1934 putsch in Austria, the Nazis' first goal was the Vienna radio station.

(Top and middle) A commemorative stamp and poster for the Volkswagen campaign. Germans were asked to pay out five marks a week for a "People's Car" which was never delivered. (Bottom) Goebbels regarded broadcasting as the most effective means of propaganda. "All Germany listens to the Führer with the People's Radio;" a poster advertising the cheap wireless set produced by the Nazis.

The Nazis made good use of short-wave transmissions to the Americas. Here a different technique was required from the blustering methods and language employed for Austria. The aim was to impress the North and South Americans with the good fellowship of Nazi Germany, and the speakers contrived an atmosphere of cozy chumminess with the listeners. They often addressed a local town or school and sent greetings to individual listeners. Intimacy was also fostered by reading these listeners' letters and answering their questions about the New Germany. Later, the globe was, for foreign broadcasting, divided into six "culture areas": North America, South America, Africa, East Asia, South Asia, and Australia. From 14 hours weekly in 1933, foreign broadcasts rose to 58 hours in 1939. Daily, 130 German transmitters broadcast 180 foreign news programs in 53 languages.

The radio, which Nazi fuglemen had early described as "the towering herald of National Socialism," soon came to be regarded as the principal propaganda medium. Neither Italy nor the Soviet Union, the other totalitarian countries, used it to such a degree on their less literate populations.

That the Party knew it owed its success to the spoken rather than the written word was neatly summed up in a directive by Goebbels to the German newspapers on how to write: "The reader should feel that you are in reality a speaker standing beside him." The pages of the Nazi newspapers therefore exuded the atmosphere of mass meetings, sweat, leather, and bloodlust; and the Party newspaper, the *Völkischer Beobachter*, became virtually no more than a glorified poster masquerading as a newspaper.

It was originally owned by Hitler's crony and wartime sergeant, Max Amman, and edited by the drunken, drug-addicted Nazi poet, Dietrich Eckart. In those days it had only 127,000 readers; but after 1933 its circulation leapt at the rate of 100,000 annually until, in 1942, it became the first German newspaper to top the million mark. That it was compulsory reading for Party members was partly responsible for this phenomenal growth. But also, civil servants, schoolteachers and the like could not obtain preferment unless they knew what was in it. A university professor got into serious trouble for giving a low grade to the essay of a student who had lifted it entirely from the columns of the *Völkischer Beobachter*. Hitler once said that the *Völkischer Beobachter* was nothing more than a humor sheet. Conversely, he called *Die Brennessel (The Nettle)*, the Party humor magazine published in Munich, "the dreariest rag imaginable." *Die Brennessel* featured the cartoons of Seppla (Josef Plank), which were vitriolic attacks on the British, Americans, and Russians.

For controlling the press, *Sprachregelungen* (language rulings) were issued daily by Goebbels' ministry to editors all over the country. When they had read them, they were instructed to destroy them and sign an affidavit to that effect. By 1939, these directives had become so detailed that the papers were virtually written for the editors, who by then offered no opposition. In a moment of candor, Goebbels admitted in his journal (April 14, 1943), "Any man with the slightest spark of honor left in him will take good care in the future not to become a journalist."

The *Sprachregelungen* dealt with almost every aspect of German life. To take a few at random: Thomas Mann was not to be written about, because his name had "been removed from the national consciousness." The same for Charles Chaplin. On the other hand, Greta Garbo and the Duke of Windsor, who had shown certain positive sentiments, were to be treated in a sympathetic manner. Photographs of ministers of the Third Reich and high Party officials attending sumptuous banquets were forbidden. No reference was to be made to a case of cattle poisoning due to excess potassium in cattle fodder; nor to an auto accident in which Ribbentrop and his daughter had been hurt; nor was Frau Hess to be shown at the Berlin dog show.

Quantitatively as well as qualitatively, the national press declined. When the Nazis came to power, there were 4,500 newspapers reflecting a variety of political persuasions. By 1939, the number had been reduced to 1,000, all of which were following the Party line.

About literature and theater as forms of propaganda in Germany there is less to say. Literature is addressed primarily to the intellect and has little mass appeal. In the words of the Nazi writer Schunzel, "In this land we do not read books. We swim, we wrestle, we lift weights." Theater too is addressed to a relatively small audience. These art forms took a minor place in the Nazi scheme of propaganda.

Most writers and dramatists of any merit had left the country or were proscribed when the Nazis came to power; men like Thomas Mann, Remarque, Zweig, Reinhardt, Toller, Brecht, Franz Werfel. The place of these "degenerates and racial undesirables" was taken by writers who turned out books and plays on the prescribed Nazi themes. Most of what has been said about the cinema applied to them. Plays had to be submitted for approval to the Reich Theater Chamber, whose task, according to the Theater Law of 1934, was "to watch the production from the point of view of conformity of its spiritual content with National Socialism." Even the German classics, plays by Goethe and Schiller, were given a nationalist flavor and their universal or humanist values attenuated. Of foreign writers, those like Bernard Shaw were approved, not for any literary merit, but because they pilloried what were regarded as the vices of English hypocrisy and "plutocracy." Hanns Johst, president of the Reich Theater Chamber, had once publicly boasted that whenever someone mentioned the word "culture" to him he wanted to reach for his revolver.

During the twelve years of Nazi rule not a single playwright of any consequence emerged. It was the heyday of the third- and fourth-rate writer; and the principal themes for books and plays were historical, the favorite subjects being medieval Germany and the rise of Prussia. A popular theme in literature was the *Fronterlebnis* (life at the front), as in the novels of Beumelberg;

(Below) Seppla (Josef Plank) mocked Churchill in this cartoon for Die Brennessel. *During the victorious phase of the war, Goebbels made Churchill his personal enemy and heaped scorn on him. After the German defeat at Stalingrad, Goebbels paid an indirect compliment to Churchill by basing his 'total war' speech on the Prime Minister's "blood, sweat, and tears" address of 1940.*

(Top) Der Angriff (The Attack) *was the weekly newspaper launched by Goebbels in 1927 when he was Gauleiter of Berlin. Goebbels used the paper to attack his enemies in the Weimar government. After 1930, Der Angriff became the daily vehicle for Goebbels' propaganda. (Bottom)* Der Stürmer, *edited by Julius Streicher, first appeared in Nuremberg in 1923 shortly after the Munich putsch. It was the most viciously anti-Semitic of the Nazi papers.*

scenes alternate between brutal descriptions of trench warfare and bathetic "comradeship" in the Teutonic sentimental style. Among other popular fictional themes was the *Heimatroman* or regional novel. Typical of these was Kunkel's *Ein Arzt sucht seinen Weg (A Doctor Seeks His Way)*, in which a restless undergraduate forsakes the medical school in the great city where he is studying to return to the hearth of his shepherd grandfather, whose life he attempts to imitate. He finishes as an herbalist effecting miraculous cures.

Another literary favorite was the Führer-type biography. It did not deal directly with Hitler, but with historical characters whose careers were made to resemble his. Thus, the biographies of the poet Schiller, the alchemist Paracelsus and the inventor Diesel, illustrate the triumph of untutored genius over formal learning, of intuition over intelligence.

All creative artists had to belong to the appropriate department of the Reich Chamber of Culture, which was founded in September, 1933. The chamber could expel or refuse entry for "political unreliability," which meant in practice that even artists who were lukewarm about National Socialism could be prevented from practicing their art. On May 10, 1933, in Berlin's Franz Jozef Platz, the notorious "burning of the books" occurred. The works of the "decadent" writers—Freud, Marx, and Zweig among them—were thrown on a ceremonial bonfire and Goebbels made a speech relayed by all German radio stations, in which he referred to the authors as "the evil spirit of the past" and declared that "the age of intellectualism" was now over.

To conclude, what lessons can be learned from the Nazi use of propaganda during the period 1933–1939? The most important, if not the most conspicuous, concerns its influence over youth. If after only six years of power Goebbels' propaganda could convince the adult masses to believe in their Führer as they did, what effect would it have had on the next generation, the youth of Germany? Had Germany won the Second World War, these young people could have spent their entire lives under the spell of a system invented and perfected by Goebbels. Fortunately, the other nations, who had fallen behind both militarily and in the practice of propaganda, quickly gained ground as soon as Hitler sprang his war on them. Because their propaganda, both to their own people and to the Germans, was based on the truth, it gradually became, as the long and testing years of war unrolled, more credible, more effective, and finally more successful, than that of Dr. Goebbels.

It is no small measure of Goebbels' skill that in 1939 he could manipulate German public opinion like a seesaw. One day in August of that year, the Germans were dutifully acknowledging that Soviet Russia was the enemy of mankind; the next day (August 24, 1939), that it was their friend and ally. Goebbels maintained this image of friendship while the Soviets were swallowing large tracts of Eastern Europe—half of Poland, the Baltic states, Bessarabia, and northern Bukovina. This he did as long as it suited Hitler's strategic requirements. When these changed with the Nazi invasion of the Soviet Union in June 1941, he switched back; bolshevism again became the bogeyman of Europe. All the anti-Soviet literature which had vanished from the German book shops in August 1939 appeared on the shelves again. This manipulation is of course relatively easy in a dictatorship. All the same, even Stalin—himself no mean propagandist—thought the Nazis went too far when they wanted to include in the nonaggression pact of August 1939 a passage about "Russo-German friendship," after, as Stalin said, they had for fifteen years been covering him with "pails of manure."

In 1939 the German people did not want war, but they had been so conditioned to the idea since 1933, and to that of their own military and racial superiority, that they accepted it without demur. When war was declared, Goebbels could proudly boast that the situation was quite different from 1914. Then, the German leadership had no idea of how to influence public opinion. But today, on September 1, 1939, "Germany knows," he wrote, "how to handle the weapon of truth with sovereign certainty."

Until the war, Goebbels' handling of "the weapon of truth" about England and France had been somewhat ambivalent. While despising "the decadent democracies" and satirizing them in such humorous papers as *Simplicissimus* and *Die Brennessel* he had, following his leader's directions, also attempted from time to time to court them. He had even referred to some of England's empire-building virtues in his papers. At the Olympic Games in 1936, he had instructed his department to treat important British visitors with respect. But now that was all over. In the winter of 1939–40, he told the Germans by press, radio, and film how perfidious and Machiavellian were the countries which had declared war on Germany. England was depicted as a citadel of "plutocracy," where a handful of corrupt financiers, most of them Jews, encouraged international warfare, because it increased their wealth, as well as their hold over the poor workingman. The Germans had no quarrel with the English masses, he said, only with their rulers. He instructed his ministry: "Our aim must be the separation of people and government in England." It was relatively easy for him to show the Germans who was responsible for the war. Britain and France had encouraged Polish "intransigence," for their own ends; it was they who had declared war on Germany, not vice versa. Germany had no alternative but to defend herself. Goebbels was even able to convince the public in April and May of 1940 that the German occupations of Denmark, Norway, Holland, and Belgium were defensive measures, taken in time to forestall the invasion of those countries by England and France, whose plans to use them as pawns had, fortunately, fallen into German hands.

The principal aim of Goebbels' propaganda in the first two years of the war, when Germany was everywhere victorious, was to convince the people that the Greater Reich which the Führer was building would benefit them all, and in the long run all of Europe. For this he had plenty of material. By the autumn of 1941, the rich corn lands of the Ukraine were in German hands;

(Top) Emil Jannings played a Boer hero in Hans Steinhoff's anti-British film, Ohm Krüger (1941). The English are depicted as greedy expansionists, anxious to possess the Transvaal gold fields. They trick Krüger when he visits London and is presented to the queen who is portrayed as a clever old harridan addicted to whisky. Krüger, on the other hand, has the mystique of a great national leader. (Bottom) Erich Waschruck's Die Rothschilds was one of several virulent anti-Semitic films which appeared in 1940. It flopped at the box office.

it was self-evident that German farmers and settlers would make two blades grow where the Slav could produce only one. Russia and its great steppes could feed a continent, if the land were "properly" cultivated and exploited. The Propaganda Ministry was inundated with requests from soldiers about how to obtain land in the Crimea or Caucasus, and settle there when the war was over. Then there was the overgorged British Empire, also ripe for plucking. With German troops nearing the Suez canal, the vast British territories in Africa, as well as the Indian subcontinent itself, beckoned.

In those early days of the war, the documentary campaign films, made in Poland, Norway, and the Low Countries, played an important part in exalting German morale. Cameramen were attached to the fighting units and accompanied them into battle, of which they gave a factual, if slanted, picture. This bias was described in 1940 by a Nazi journalist, Hans-Joachim Giese, whose comments about newsreels also held true for the campaign documentaries: "The newsreel does not, in its fulfillment of the precept of propaganda, represent truth in itself—for that would be senseless and not even within its power—but rather, with proper expedients, the newsreel represents just that aspect of the truth which of necessity ought to be spread in the interest of the German nation." Although Goebbels would have put it more succinctly, this sums up the essence of Nazi propaganda.

Baptism of Fire, a documentary about the Polish campaign, was shown simultaneously in 55 movie houses in Berlin, and throughout the Reich. Mobile film vans took it to remote villages which lacked movie theaters. In this and other films, the horrors of war were always shown as being visited on the resisting army, never on the German troops. So important were these films considered that in 1940, a law was passed forbidding anyone from leaving or entering a theater during the showing of a war documentary.

In this period of military victories, the task of the Propaganda Ministry was relatively easy. Victories are the best form of propaganda, and the army communiqués did most of Goebbels' work for him. This did not entirely please him, because the Supreme Command of the Wehrmacht took over, as it were, a part of his traditional role. In war, the demands of military secrecy hampered the use of propaganda as he understood it. He even said, "Hitler will soon be listening to his generals only, and it will be very difficult for me." However, it at least enabled him to turn his attention for a while to propaganda for the enemy.

Already in the "phony war" of 1939–40 the Propaganda Ministry was organizing broadcasts to France, sowing discord between the Western Allies. The French were told that the British had sent only six divisions, and that the eighty French divisions would have to bear the brunt of the fighting. The British, as usual, would fight "to the last Frenchman." Leaflets, such as the famous "Falling Leaf," were dropped by air on the French troops in the Maginot line, describing how the British army in the Lille area was ravishing their wives and sweethearts. From Stuttgart a French traitor, Ferdonnet, broadcast to France lurid

BEFREIER

..Wir kämpfen für das Kultur, Jimmy."
..Ja - aber was ist Kultur eigentlich?"

accounts of corruption in the French government and Jewish high finance. There was always an element of truth in these allegations; for as Charles Roetter, the English expert on wartime propaganda, says, "It must strike a chord that is always there." To his own people, Goebbels depicted the French as "a dying nation," a highly talented but unfortunate people at the end of their political tether, "becoming more and more negroidal."

To sow dissension in the British camp, Goebbels set up the so-called "Scottish transmitter," with dialect broadcasts on the English iniquities in Scotland and Ireland, and the English habit throughout history of enlisting Scottish and Irish regiments to fight their battles for them. The heartlessness of the "plutocratic" English upper classes was also proved, he said, during the Battle of France. Thousands of Frenchmen were dying daily, but the British aristocrats went on the first Wednesday of June to watch their horses racing in the Derby. Just how much effect this propaganda had is uncertain. It undoubtedly had some influence on the collapse of the French army, but the broadcasts of traitors like William Joyce, "Lord Haw-Haw," were never taken seriously in England.

A month after the German invasion of the Soviet Union, Goebbels set up a secret radio station broadcasting to the Soviets, calling itself "Leninist" and purporting to be from within Russia. Its speaker was one Albrecht, a Russian of German origin who had fled to Germany after Stalin's 1936 purges. He voiced the popular discontent in Russia with the Stalinist regime. Goebbels established a similar operation for North America. When it seemed that America's sympathies were inclining more and more toward England, a "black" radio station purporting to be in America was set up in Germany broadcasting isolationist propaganda to the United States.

Both Goebbels and Hitler believed that their anti-Semitic and anti-Bolshevik propaganda, as served up for home consumption, had only to be repeated abroad to have the same effect. Here they were wrong. Neither before nor during the war did anti-Semitism prove a good article of export. The endless tirades against the Jews in Germany lost the sympathies of many English and Americans who were not particularly pro-Jewish. This can be explained in part by the Nazis' ignorance of foreign countries. Neither Hitler nor Goebbels had traveled much outside Germany, and they knew no foreign languages. For rulers of the most powerful military nation in the world, now at war, their ignorance about their adversaries is truly staggering. In the winter of 1940 they believed that their anti-Churchill propaganda to Britain would soon make the British realize that Churchill was responsible for their sufferings, and that they would dismiss him. In his "Table Talk" Hitler reveals this. "Churchill," he said, "is a typical big mouth, and an incompetent drunkard—in his private life not a gentleman either." Goebbels was equally preposterous about Anthony Eden. "The perfumed British foreign secretary," he wrote in his diary, "cuts a good figure among these characters from the synagogue. His

(Top) William Joyce, known as Lord Haw-Haw, was a turncoat Englishman who broadcast Nazi propaganda to his countrymen from Germany. After war was declared, Britons ceased to take him seriously. (Bottom) As part of Goebbels' anti-Semitic campaign, photographs of Eastern European ghetto Jews were distributed to newspapers by the Propaganda Ministry.

(Top) A British photograph of Churchill inspecting a new machine gun. (Bottom) "Churchill, a sniper;" a 1941 German poster which used the same photograph of the Prime Minister with his head cocked at an angle.

whole education and his entire bearing can be characterized as thoroughly Jewish." These comments are revealing of the inferiority complex and jealous hatred by the upstart, whose power has gone to his head, for the aristocrat.

Once the power of the German army had been established in the Polish campaign, Goebbels did not bother much about the susceptibilities of any foreigners he wished to influence. On April 5, 1940, a number of important Danes and Norwegians, politicians and businessmen, were invited to the German embassy in Oslo, where they were shown the film *Baptism of Fire*, in which the futility of the Polish resistance to the German army is graphically depicted. Five days later, the German army invaded Denmark and Norway.

Baptism of Fire, Feldzug im Polen (Campaign in Poland), and later those films of the campaigns in Scandinavia, the Low Countries, and France, such as *Sieg im Westen (Victory in the West)*, were sent to German embassies all over the world for distribution to local movie houses. The public in Ankara, Sofia, the South American countries, even China, were to become aware of the invincibility of the Wehrmacht. Why, the films seemed to ask, should other cities have to suffer the fate of Warsaw? Why should so many young men be killed to no purpose? It was better not to be an enemy of Germany. As the Germans invaded country after country, these propaganda techniques were extended to occupied territories. Occupied Europe became a monopoly market for Goebbels' films and traveling exhibitions.

In those years of victory, when Goebbels had less work at the ministry, he threw himself hecticly into every other form of war work. He toured armament factories in the Ruhr and gave pep talks to dockers in Hamburg; he received delegations of Japanese Youth leaders, Spanish publishers, Dutch poets. Everything interested him, from the price of potatoes to the sexual needs of the foreign workers in Germany. He personally directed the publication of a fictional diary recording the pornographic experiences of a British soldier in France, for distribution in that country. And in a particularly brilliant propaganda coup, Goebbels had the same *wagon-lit* in which Germany had surrendered to France in 1918 brought to Compiègne in 1940 for the French surrender to Hitler.

One element of home propaganda which remained completely in his hands was the Führer legend. Before the war, he had shown Hitler as the wise and sober statesman; now, the Führer was presented as the great strategist and military genius who, in spite of the pessimistic warnings of his generals, had shattered the entire French army in a month. He was a clairvoyant with the prophetic gift of a seer—a universal man, an expert in all military techniques, intimately familiar with the workings of every tank and machine gun. Films were shown of him in his Field Headquarters. The camera would catch a group of deliberating generals, then move slowly to a table where the Führer stood alone poring over the map of Russia, his face charged with worry and the burden of his thoughts. "There he stands!" wrote Goebbels in his paper, "Planning the future. Utterly great and utterly lonely!"

However this "universal genius," for whom nothing went wrong between 1933 and 1941, suddenly ran into trouble. Although in 1942 still in possession of most of Europe—from the Don to the Spanish frontier, from Norway to the Greek isles—he found he had, as Napoleon had 140 years before, brought into existence against him one of the greatest coalitions the world has ever seen. His run of successes was halted. It was now that propaganda in the sense that Goebbels understood it—influencing public opinion—came into its own again. Between 1939 and 1941, German public opinion had needed no influencing. The roar of the tanks at Sedan, the scream of the diving Stukas at Dunkirk, had muffled the voice of Goebbels. But now as the blows of the Allies began to fall on Germany, all those skills were called upon again. Propaganda came into its own with the first German defeats. Goebbels had to compensate for the failure of the German army. And this he did in the greatest propaganda exercise of his life.

He addressed himself first to the unfortunate German troops who by the winter of 1941–42 were not victorious, as expected, in Muscovite billets, but sitting in the snow and ice outside the Soviet capital in the worst winter for fifty years. No provision had been made for this; in fact, the overconfident troops were wearing summer uniforms. Goebbels immediately inaugurated his *Winterhilfesspende*, a collection throughout the Reich of winter clothing for the troops. For the first time he had to admit that the estimate of a short campaign had proved incorrect. He could no longer continue the line of infallibility. The Nazis, like other human beings, he admitted, could make mistakes. But for that very reason, everyone must now work harder for victory. The Russian soldier, he explained, had proved to be a tougher fighter than expected (he was careful to add that it was purely animal toughness, in this blunted human material, and should not be confused with valor). There was an immediate response to his appeal for warm clothing from all over Germany. For weeks, the collections took first place in the public mind. Athletes and film stars were engaged to make patriotic speeches at them. All Germany contributed, both men and women offering everything from their mink coats to their woolen underwear. In fact, the collection came a little late for the troops in Russia, when most of the winter was over; but it proved an excellent means of strengthening the links between the home and the fighting fronts which—Goebbels had noted in his diary—were, after the run of constant successes, not as close as they should be.

In the summer and autumn of 1942 German forces had one more victorious spell, advancing as far as the Caucasus and Stalingrad. Again the communiqués told their joyous tale. But it was the last time. In October of that year came defeat at El Alamein, immediately followed by the Anglo-American landings in North Africa, and the great Soviet victory at Stalingrad.

Goebbels was instantly at work. When the German army was expelled from Africa in 1943, he explained it in his paper *Das Reich* as a peripheral affair. "What happens in North Africa,"

(*Top*) On May 23, 1944, British and American troops launched a successful offensive against the Germans from the Anzio beachhead in Italy. This leaflet was intended by German propagandists to lower Allied morale. (*Middle*) Another leaflet showered on the Allied forces in Italy as they advanced northward in 1944. (*Bottom*) "To the Honorary Headhunter in the White House," a cartoon from the humor magazine Kladderdatsch.

Dem Ehrenkopfjäger im Weißen Haus

(Top) An advertisement encouraging
Germans to observe the weekly "one
pot" meal to conserve food, especially
meat. The text reads, "the meal of
sacrifice for the Reich." (Bottom)
"The correct mask position protects
your health;" a poster exhorting people
to wear their gas masks during
bombing raids.

he scoffed, "is absolutely unimportant. It is on the rim of Europe. The war will be decided in Europe." Even when the Allies invaded Sicily and established a foothold on the Italian mainland, the news was given little prominence in the German press and radio, compared with the battles in Russia.

To explain away Stalingrad was a harder task; but Goebbels made a brave attempt. The 300,000 dead there were all now heroes in Valhalla; their action had not been in vain. For several months they had held up the assault of six Soviet armies who would otherwise now be rampaging across the Don. On February 18, 1943, he summoned an enormous rally at the Sportpalast in Berlin to explain this. He worked up the thousands who had been specially selected to be present—by virtue of their sure "spontaneous" reactions—into a frenzy of patriotic hysteria. "The Germans," he shrieked, "have been inwardly purified by the blow of fate that fell on them at Stalingrad. It has given them the new strength they require for victory." The vast audience bayed their approval. His two-hour harangue was relayed over all the radio stations so that it, and the vociferous mob, might influence unseen millions both at home and abroad. The doubters and waverers, hearing the audience's reaction to Stalingrad and imagining it to be representative of all Germany, were to be reassured, as were foreigners, by the impression of a nation united as never before. This meeting, in which Goebbels demanded "Total War," was one of his masterpieces of mass propaganda.

But nothing he said could hold up the Soviet tide. By now the Red armies had taken the initiative, and all along the 1000-mile front the Germans were in retreat. A new note now sounded in Goebbels' propaganda. Until Stalingrad, he had always represented Nazi Germany as "The New Order" in Europe, young and vital, supplanting the old, effete, reactionary European systems which had been governing it for too long. The pre-1933 Europe, Goebbels had constantly proclaimed, was finished, tired out. Good riddance to it! No mention was made of Europe's glorious past, of the works of art and literature which had made this "effete system" for centuries the wonder of the world. Now with "the barbarian hordes advancing from the East," Goebbels depicted Nazi Germany as the defender of all that was sacred and traditional in Europe, the sole bastion of Western civilization against "the Slavonic flood"; in his own words, "Always Prusso-Germany has been the wall against which the Eastern hordes were crushed. Today, Germany stands guard for the whole of Europe." The Russians were depicted as subhumans to whom a Gothic cathedral was a place for stabling horses. To show what these barbarians looked like, he published photographs of Russian prisoners of war taken after long forced marches or days in suffocating cattle trucks, arriving in Germany in such a state of emaciation that they indeed looked subhuman. In 1942 a traveling exhibition entitled "Europa gegen den Bolshewismus" (Europe against Bolshevism) was sent around all occupied Europe. Anti-Bolshevik films such as Village in the Red Storm revealed the alleged inhumanity of the

Soviets to their own people.

Here Goebbels played on the Germans' traditional feelings about the Russians, which had been strong in Germany long before the name Hitler had ever been heard—a mixture of superiority complex and fear. If the Russians penetrated into Germany, he warned, the young German manhood would be carried off to Siberia, while her womanhood would be delivered to the lust of savages from the steppes. All German males would be sterilized, the children separated from their mothers and deported. He was much helped in this propaganda at the time by the Allies' unconditional surrender demand, which convinced the Germans that they would obtain no mercy from the Allies. He quoted foreign newspaper reports that Soviet Russia would immediately take 10 million German males to rebuild their country. Every German was aware of the centuries of conflict between Teuton and Slav, an awareness most favorable to the propagandist. Similar apprehension about the West, Britain and France, could not be stimulated because there was no national tradition to nourish them. The theme "Europe as a Russian slave camp," which Goebbels played on right up to the end, was undoubtedly effective in keeping the Germans fighting. "Strength through Fear" he called it.

It was now that Allied propaganda to Germany presented Goebbels with a new difficulty. As long as the Wehrmacht was triumphant, Allied propaganda could have little effect. In the first years of the war, the BBC could do no more than repeat, "We will be back," a slogan regarded by most Germans in 1940 and 1941 as ludicrous. Allied propaganda was a late starter, but when the German defeats began in October 1942, it was quick to take advantage of them. Goebbels had said that the expulsion of the Germans from Africa was of "the smallest importance because it is peripheral," and he had naturally not mentioned how many German troops were taken prisoner in Tunisia. The BBC quoted this back and then asked, was it of small importance to lose a quarter of a million men? And then there were the *Sondermeldungen,* the special announcements which had made such a stir at the time of the German victories. With a fanfare, the latest victory would be proudly announced over the radio, the fall of each capital of Europe: Paris, Belgrade, Athens, Kiev, etc., and all the victorious battles. The German people would remember the broadcasts, said the BBC. There had been 65 *Sondermeldungen* in 1941. In 1942, there had been 19. In 1943, only two. What did this mean?

The BBC also began to play back the speeches made by the German leaders in their hours of victory. On October 25, 1940, Goebbels had made a great speech claiming that England was already beaten. This speech was played back verbatim on the German service of the BBC, with the comment that three years later England seemed to be alive and kicking—witness the holocaust the RAF had just caused in Hamburg. Goering's speech in 1940 was also replayed: "We shall not allow a single enemy bomb to fall on the Ruhr." Three nights prior, Essen had been almost obliterated by British bombs. Hitler's speech in 1941,

(Top, left and right) British "black" propaganda parodies of the Winter Relief charity stamps issued by the German Post Office. Himmler solicits contributions at gunpoint and a German soldier is shown with his face shot off while Nazi officers offer a toast in the background. (Bottom) British "black" parody of a German stamp. 30 January 1933 was the day Hitler became Chancellor. Himmler is placing leg cuffs on a manacled civilian who represents the German people.

(Below and opposite page) Several pages from the British book Truffle Eater, *by Oistros, published in 1940. The book was a sophisticated form of propaganda for an audience who could joke about the Nazis even in the midst of war.*

Shock-Troop Headed Adolf

Look at Adolf where he stands
With his Nazi hair and hands,
Murmuring beneath his breath
Like the lady of Macbeth,
As he seeks in vain to blot,
What he sees : " Out damnéd spot."
But though rather like a tweeny
In the clothes of Mussolini,
Adolf, you can shelter when in
Doubt, behind your uncle Lenin.

"the Soviet Union is already destroyed and will never rise again," was also played back; it was immediately followed with detailed figures about the German casualties at Stalingrad. Incidentally, asked the BBC, what had happened to Hitler? He had never stopped speechifying in 1940 and 1941. Now he had become silent. He had not made a public speech for over a year. Could it be that he was ashamed of something?

Goebbels was equal to this last one. He answered haughtily and with a hypocrisy which was exceptional even for him, "The Führer stands in contrast to the commonplace figures on the other side, who lose no opportunity of displaying themselves before the footlights of the world stage." Men of true historic caliber, he said, did not need the unstable approval of publicity. Their strength sprang from the demon of their historic mission, which they fulfilled according to a higher law.

That the BBC broadcasts were based on the truth soon became apparent to listeners all over the continent. In Germany itself, as the military situation deteriorated the clandestine audience grew so large that severe penalties were imposed for listening to Allied radio; in Goebbels' words; "it is for a civilian as despicable as for the soldier who commits self-mutilation." The *Volksempfänger* was so constructed that it could tune in to only one or two German stations. Yet though lacking short wave, it could tune in to the powerful BBC transmitter on medium wave. At one point, when listening to the BBC in the occupied countries had also increased alarmingly, the Nazis considered confiscating all wireless sets; but the plan was abandoned (except in Holland), because the Germans would thereby lose a valuable instrument for their own propaganda. The radio, which Goebbels had used in such masterly fashion during the '30s, was now being turned against him.

In the last years of the war, Josef Goebbels continued his activities relentlessly. While the other Nazi leaders gradually realized the hopelessness of the situation, and withdrew into silence or secret negotiations with the enemy, the little doctor became more belligerent and chauvinistic. Every instrument of propaganda which came to hand he eagerly seized. When the V-1 and V-2 secret weapons were being constructed, he organized a "whispering campaign" about them. The public morale was to be lifted by stories that the new V weapons were unanswerable and that when they were put to use London would be entirely destroyed in 48 hours. He encouraged rumors about a new U-boat which could travel submerged at such speeds that it could chase the British battle squadrons around the Atlantic, sinking them one by one; and about a special anti-aircraft cannon whose missiles were magnetically drawn to the aircraft in the sky. All this made people feel better.

After the 1944 invasion of Normandy, the German people were shown films which undeniably revealed British troops being driven back into the sea, leaving quantities of dead and wounded. In fact, the films were of the British failure in Dieppe two years earlier. Then there was the Katyn incident, where some 2,000 corpses of Polish officers murdered by the Russians

The Story of Adolf Head-in-Air

As he trudged along to be
Europe's Man of Destiny,
Adolf always kept his eye
Vaguely fixed upon the sky,
Far too much preoccupied
To decide
In what streets he walked about,
Or to hear the children shout:
" Look at little Adolf there—
Little Adolf Head-in-Air."

First, when walking on a wharf,
He encountered Ludendorff.
Adolf's gaze was souf and norf,
Floating high
In the sky,
And he did not hear the cry
" You'll be sorry bye and bye."
Ouch !
Putsch !

With his head as high as ever,
Much too clever to be clever,
Adolf watched the eagle's eyries,
For the wings of the Valkyries,
Having guessed
That it may be cleverest
Just to dream and not to look
(*Vide* Joseph in the Book),
Leaving lads like Roehm and Goebbels
To attend to daily troubles,
While Big Business and the Yunkers
Picked his ball out of the bunkers,
And then laid it
On the green, and swore they'd played it,
With no shame or that or thisness,
Trust the Junkers and Big Business.

Like a picture etched by Dürer,

The Story of Baby Goering

Baby, Baby Goering !
Mother's simply purring.
Father's gone to shoot a Yid
To make a supper for his kid.

The Story of Goering who would not have the Jews

Goering, looking like a cherry
In a glass of grocer's sherry,
From his fingers to his frown,
All synthetically brown
Used to spend his time in Sweden
For his private reasons hidden.
But, returning home one day,
Screamed " O, take the Jews away,
Take the nasty Jews away,
I won't have any Jews to-day."

Kind Mama, discreetly purring,
Thus addresses bully Goering :
" Child, in the all seeing plan
For the chosen Aryan,
Jews exist to give the Teuton
Something he can wipe his boot on.
There, no doubt, are other toys
Suitable for German boys,
Such as soldiers and guns
And the history of the Huns.
But the Jews so beautifully
Fit the purpose of the bully,
That to banish all the vermin
Positively is un-German."

Will he listen ? He will not,
" If I were the lieber Gott
(As cocaine suggests I am),
I would smear the tribe like jam,

The Story of the Boy
who went out to Burn the Books

This is the boy who burns the books,
This is the way he always looks,
As though his mind were made of suet,
And this is the way he went to do it.

He washed his eyes with yellow soap,
He stole his father's microscope,
For books are books and the law is law,
And he had to be sure of what he saw.

(And meantime mild angelic eyes
Smiled amiably in Paradise
At this attempt to change the plans
Of Heaven's own librarians).

Then, like a spaniel in a fog,
He snuffles through a catalogue,
Slowly, because he has to spell
It syllable by syllable.

Theology, of course, is banned,
With metaphysics out of hand,
Because all these are merely views
Of Social Democrats and Jews.

Next he destroys what seems to him in
The worst of taste—all books by women,
Who actually write as if
Thought weren't man's prerogative.

But when he contemplates the novel
He needs an automatic shovel,
To clear a path through the abysm
Of post-armistice pacificism.

in 1940 were discovered by the Germans in a trench in east Poland. By giving this great publicity, Goebbels managed to cause the first rift in the Grand Alliance, between the Polish government-in-exile in London and Soviet Russia. "How clever we are," he boasted, "to have converted the Katyn affair into a highly political question." To the end, he believed that this rift would result in England and America dissociating themselves from the alliance with the Soviet Union because, in his words, it was "so unnatural."

His active part in crushing the Officers' Plot of July 20, 1944 to assassinate Hitler is well enough known. His propaganda about it afterwards was most ingenious. By insisting on the incompetence and cowardice of these brave men, he successfully diminished their stature in the eyes of their countrymen. He was even able to persuade the German people that the whole episode was beneficial, evidence that the hand of providence was behind the Führer. After it, he coined the slogan "Hitler ist der Sieg" (Hitler is Victory). Then late in 1944, when it was clear that the war was lost, he made his last attempt to stimulate the flagging morale by producing a film about the Napoleonic wars in which the besieged Prussian city of Kolberg fought to the last man, and was saved by a military miracle. The lesson was clear. But no military lessons, nor miracles, could now save "the New Germany." On April 30, 1945, after naming Goebbels chancellor, Hitler committed suicide in his Berlin bunker. After an unsuccessful attempt to negotiate with the Soviets, Goebbels shot his wife, six children, and himself on the next day, May 1, 1945, exactly one week before the Allied victory in Europe.

Most nations will stop fighting when they have given up all hope of victory. It is Goebbels' supreme achievement that, by his sinister art, he persuaded the Germans to continue fighting long after they had abandoned all hope.

"Who is the most important man in the world?"
National Socialist election poster, 1932/Germany/Artist unknown.

National Socialist election poster, 1932/
Germany/Photomontage by Heinrich Hoffman.

"The flag bearer," 1930s/Germany/
Hubert Lanzinger.

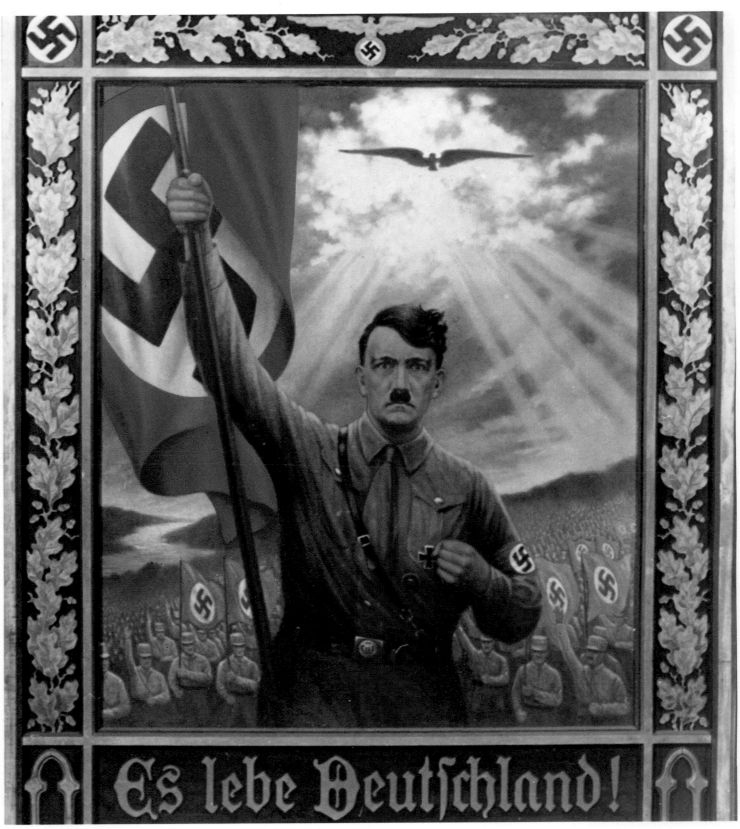

"Germany lives," 1930s/
Germany/K. Stauber.

Hitler had no use for intellectuals like Einstein,
c. 1933/Germany/Seppla (Josef Plank).

The Nazis sweep out alien elements, early 1930s/
Germany/Seppla (Josef Plank).

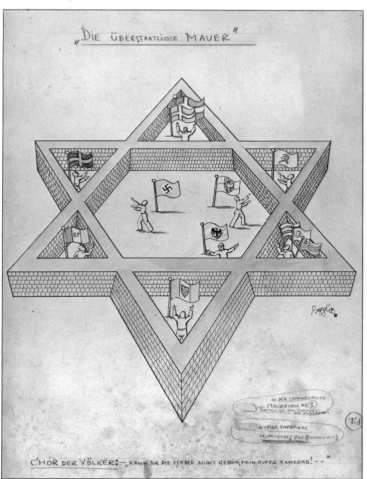

"The wall between nations," no date/Germany/
Seppla (Josef Plank).

"Germany, your colonies," c. 1935/Germany/
E. Glintzer.

"World Meeting of Hitler Youth," 1935/
Germany/Ludwig Hohlwein.

Hitler Youth postcard, no date/Germany/
H. Bargher.

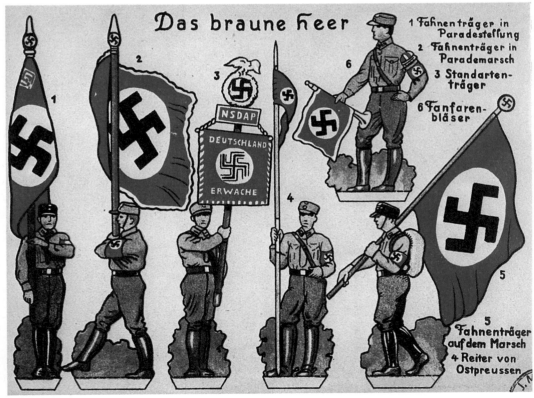

SA cutout toys, 1930s/Germany/
Artist unknown.

*"And You?" (Poster for the Stalhelm Soldier's League),
1932/Germany/Ludwig Hohlwein.*

Poster for the film Jew Süss, c. 1940/Germany/
Artist unknown.

Churchill as a greedy octopus, c. 1940/Germany/
Seppla (Josef Plank).

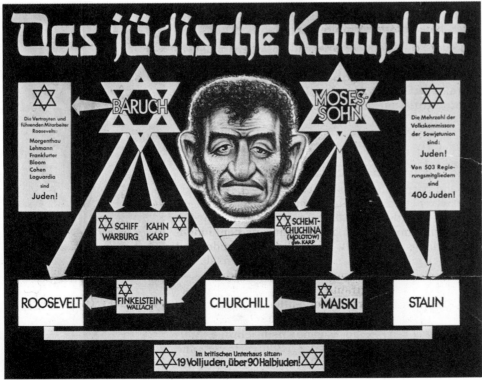

"The Jewish Plot," no date/Germany/
Artist unknown.

Poster for The Eternal Jew *exhibition,*
1937/Germany/Artist unknown.

*"The German Student Fights for the Führer/and the People,"
1930's/Germany/Ludwig Hohlwein.*

*(Top) Issued to mark the Saar Plebiscite, 1934. (Middle, left)
In commemoration of the 10th anniversary of the Lufthansa
air service, 1936. (Middle, right) Commemoration of the 1935
Nazi Congress at Nuremberg. (Bottom, left) Issued to commemorate
the 12th anniversary of the first Hitler "putsch" at Munich,
1923. (Bottom, right) Issued to commemorate War Hero's Day,
1935/Germany/Artists unknown.*

*Winter Olympics, 1936/Germany/
Ludwig Hohlwein.*

*(Top) Issued in commemoration of the fifth anniversary
of the assumption of power by the Nazis, January 28, 1938/
Germany/Artist unknown. (Above) Issued in commemoration of
the Winter and Summer Olympic Games, 1936/Germany/Artist unknown.*

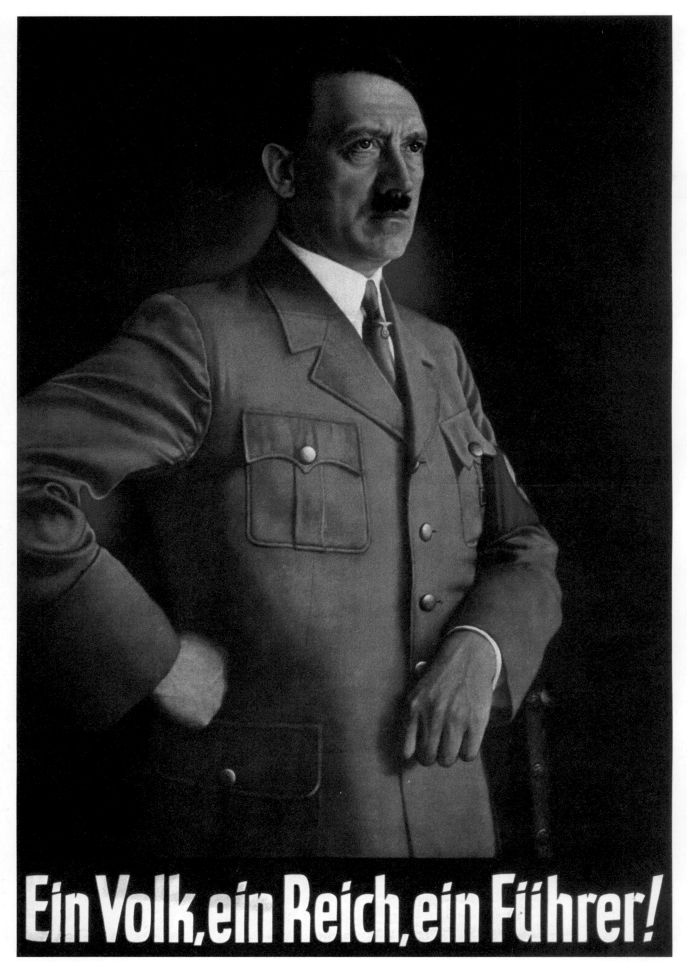

*"One people, one nation, one leader," 1938/
Germany/Artist unknown.*

"Help Hitler build. Buy German goods," 1930s/
Germany/Gunther Nagel.

"Build youth hostels and homes," 1938 or 1939/
Germany/Hermann Witte.

"Strength Through Joy Folk Festival," 1930s/
Germany/Artist unknown.

*Issued to commemorate the union of Austria with
Germany, April 10, 1938/Germany/Artist unknown.*

Issued to commemorate Grand Prix racing triumphs.
International Automobile Show, Berlin, 1939/Germany/
Artist unknown.

Issued as a reminder of Hitler's "People's Car" (the Volkswagen).
International Automobile Show, Berlin, 1939/Germany/Artist unknown.

Anti-Russian cartoon before the short-lived
peace pact, 1937/Germany/Seppla (Josef Plank).

"Bolshevism threatens when we let up; fight to victory!" c. 1942,/Germany/Artist unknown.

"Big Antibolshevik Exhibit," 1930s/Germany/ Artist unknown.

"Perfectly adapted for our flag (postcard)," c. 1942/ Germany/Artist unknown.

"Uncle Sam's economic platform," c. 1941/
Germany/Seppla (Josef Plank).

England is threatened by a Jewish Bolshevik
conspiracy, no date/Germany/Seppla (Josef Plank).

Schach dem King!

"Check to the king!" 1940/Germany/
Artist unknown.

Recruiting poster for the Waffen SS, 1941/
Germany/Anton.

Recruiting poster for the Hermann Göring
Division, 1943/Germany/Apportin.

"Victory will be ours," c. 1942/Germany/
Artist unknown.

"One struggle, one victory," 1943/Germany/
Mjölnir (Hans Schweitzer).

"Just as we fight, work for victory," c. 1942/
Germany/Rothgaengel.

"Adolf Hitler is Victory," 1943/Germany/
R. Gerhard Zill.

*Issued to commemorate the Day of Youth Obligation,
March 26, 1943/Germany/Artist unknown.*

*"SA service develops comradeship, toughness,
strength," 1941/Germany/Otto Flechtner.*

"Germany's victory, Europe's freedom," c. 1942/
Germany/Artist unknown.

Germans were warned that anyone might
spy, no date/Germany/Artist unknown.

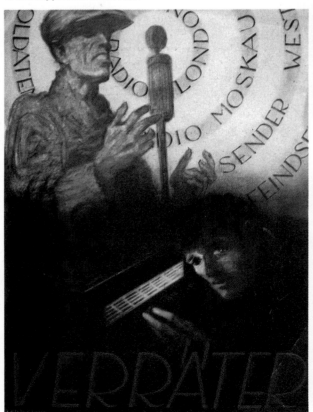

"Traitor!" 1944/Germany/
Max Spielmanns.

Model for "black" parody stamp (page 64)
1944/Germany/Artist unknown.

"Blackout! The enemy sees your light," c. 1940/
Germany/Herweg.

British "black" parody of a German stamp, no date/
England/Artist unknown.

CHAPTER TWO

MUSSOLINI'S NEW ROME
1922-1945

"Books are good, but muskets are better."
FASCIST SLOGAN

The first modern Italian propagandist was Gabriele D'Annunzio (1863–1938), the flamboyant poet and nationalist. As early as 1912 in his patriotic play *La Nave* (*The Ship*), he called for a revival of the Roman Empire. He despised the Italy he lived in, the parliamentary Italy with its unadventurous, security-seeking, property-worshipping bourgeois society. "In Latin days," he cried, "the Italian was king of all the seas, ruler of all domains to the distant horizon and the limits of empire." Like Hitler and Goebbels in Germany twenty years later, he was among the first propagandists to recognize the latent power of the masses. In *La Nave* he depicts a crowd being worked up by a skilled orator from relative apathy to collective curiosity, and thence to patriotic frenzy. A natural orator as well as a poet, D'Annunzio made impassioned speeches in 1915, inflaming the Roman masses and helping to bring Italy into the war. Later in 1919, having seized the disputed city of Fiume for Italy by a daring *coup de main*, he held it for over a year with his oratory, in face of all international opposition—including that of the Italian government.

It was his avowed intention to revive the Mediterranean past in Italy; he proclaimed, "I glory in the fact that I am a Latin, and I recognize a barbarian in every man of non-Latin blood." He thus sowed the seeds of Fascism, which Mussolini was later to reap. When the dictator came to power in 1922, the example of D'Annunzio in Fiume was still before him, and he took over all the poet's rabble-raising paraphernalia—the mob oratory, the cult of ancient Rome, the uniforms, the gun at the belt, the violence, the dialogue between orator and audience.

During the D'Annunzian occupation of Fiume, the people and the *arditi* (D'Annunzio's troops) would gather daily in the piazza before the Commandatura. The poet would come out on the balcony in his bemedalled uniform and deliver a harangue about the iniquities of the Versailles treaty, the treachery of the Allies, and the resurrection of poor, mutilated Italy under a new Roman Empire.

This was to be repeated even more theatrically in the years to come by Benito Mussolini, from the balcony of the Palazzo Venezia in Rome. He too revived the power of the piazza and enlisted the spontaneous voice of the mob. He too liked to palaver with them, and they would shout back "*Salutiamo il Duce! Fon datore dell'Impero!*" ("We salute the Duce! Founder of Empire!")—cries which reverberated across the piazza, and then over the radio to every city, town, and hamlet in Italy.

Mussolini shared D'Annunzio's scorn for the liberal Italy of the late 19th and early 20th centuries, as well as his nostalgia for the glories of ancient Rome, whose resurrection he calculated could be a powerful factor in achieving power for his party, as well as the only way of saving Italy in the modern technical world. Long before Hitler came to power, Mussolini was proclaiming that some time between 1936 and 1940, a turning point would come in European history, when a new era would be ushered in. This was remarkably prescient. He deduced that if Italy was to take advantage of this change, she must be fully

(Below) The knitted brow and pursed lips in this early-1930s caricature of the Duce express his intensity and determination. A former journalist, Mussolini knew the value of propaganda; the Fascist party continually sought affirmations of approval from the public for its policies. One leader called propaganda an instrument for the continual conquest of the masses.

armed. Armaments alone, he believed, could compensate for Italy's natural economic weakness.

To the Italian people, disillusioned by the peace treaties of 1919 and uninspired by their parliamentary leaders (men like Giolitti and Nitti who lacked entirely that bravura so dear to the Italian soul), Mussolini offered something new, as well as old— a return to the military virtues which had made Rome great. In the social and political chaos left by the First World War, with its permanent strikes and political upheaval on the left which the Italian bourgeois politicians seemed powerless to prevent, Mussolini offered hope and glory. He intended that Fascism should be not only a party, but a way of life, based on courage, discipline and self-sacrifice, such as had not been seen in Italy since the days of the elder Cato. This was later codified in the *Enciclopedia Italiana*: "The Fascist conception of the State is all-embracing. Outside it, no human or spiritual values can exist, much less have value." And Mussolini invented the graceless word *fascistizzare*, "to fascisticize," which meant applying the Fascist doctrine to all spheres of human life. To recall the modern heroic past, he used the name of Goffredo Mamelli, a patriot who fought and died for Garibaldi. This also established a link between Garibaldi's red shirts and the black ones with which Mussolini clothed his followers.

Like Hitler a man of the people, he understood the masses, particularly their admiration for violence which, as an approved weapon for the Fascists, was revealed in the symbols on the letterheads of their newspapers and pamphlets—a clenched fist, a club, a provocative jutting chin. Mussolini's use of violence between 1919 and 1922 for dealing with the communist riots was certainly effective, and brought many waverers into the Fascist camp. All over the peninsula, he organized his men into well-armed *squadristi* who simply exterminated the communists physically. Any town or village with a socialist municipality was their target. In the province of Ferrara, for example, there were twenty-one socialist councils in November 1920. By the end of 1921, all but four had disappeared, liquidated by the *squadristi* under Italo Balbo, one of Mussolini's most active lieutenants. The supine liberal governments, changing every few months, could no more curb the Fascist terror than they could control the communist-led riots. On October 28, 1922, Facta's government capitulated to Mussolini.

The absolutist regime which he now instituted was based on the theory of an elite of forceful men, not elected but in power by merit, led by a single heroic figure inspired by destiny—the Duce. One of the slogans Mussolini employed to implant this image in the Italian mind was "Caesar has come to life again in the Duce!" He had also chosen the name Fascist for its classical associations. The *fasces* were bundles of elm or birch rods from whose end projected an axe, carried in ancient Rome by the *lictors* (attendants of a magistrate); they were the insignia of official authority, symbolizing the magistrate's power to scourge and decapitate. Mussolini adopted the term in 1919, not yet as Fascist but as *fasci di combattimento*, literally "bundles for com-

(Opposite page) "Read The Fascist Worker." *All professional groups in Fascist Italy were organized, and propaganda programs were produced for each group. The swirling lines of the figure show that the Fascists, unlike the Nazis, could tolerate contemporary design. (Below, An early Fascist election poster. The young* squadrista *sounds a trumpet to awaken the sleeping conscience of the public.*

(Below) Schoolbooks, which had to be approved by the state, were rewritten to stress militaristic themes. School-children were told that "A book and a rifle make a perfect Fascist." The government created a secular rite of passage for young boys through a succession of youth groups, beginning with the "Sons of the She-Wolf" at age four and ending in the army in their late teens. The lurking shadow of a soldier behind the Balilla youth in this textbook illustration leaves little doubt that the lesson was war.

bat." These bundles became the *squadristi* who mowed down communists and other opponents.

Other devices he employed for identifying his party with ancient Rome were: the Roman salute instead of the bourgeois handshake; the use of Roman numerals for counting the years from 1922, and the initials E.F. (*Era Fascista*) instead of A.D. (thus 1929 A.D. became VII E.F.) The standards of the various Fascist leagues and organizations were modeled on the Roman *labarum* surmounted by the Imperial eagle. The ranks of the Youth Movement, the *Balilla,* bore the titles of units of the classical Roman army. The anniversaries of famous Roman political and literary figures—Caesar, Augustus, Virgil, Horace—were celebrated with great pomp. Postage stamps were issued to recall the memory of these famous men, together with other great Italians of the past: Dante, Ariosto, Tasso, da Vinci. Stamps also depicted ancient and modern ships, the former in the background, the latter in the foreground, with the motto "*Il nostro destino è stato, è sarà, sempre sul mare*" ("Our destiny has been, and will be, always on the sea"). This last was to remind Italians of their ancient Mediterranean supremacy (*mare nostrum,* "our sea"), as well as of the old Roman colonies of the North African shore, which must return to Italy. The vast monuments erected during the fascist period also contributed to the atmosphere of ancient Rome reborn—in particular the great Foro Mussolini, an imitation of the Roman forum. In a series of impassioned speeches, Mussolini informed his countrymen that the Italians were about to rule Western civilization again, after a lapse of 1500 years; and that they must discipline themselves for the conquests ahead. The Second Rome, the period of decadence, was over, to be replaced by the Third Rome, which would be as glorious as the First.

This cult of a revived Rome may be compared in contemporary Germany with the Nazi cult of the Teutonic past. The broad lines of propaganda in the two dictatorships, Italian and German, were the same—the mob oratory, the early domination of the juvenile mind, the cult of violence, exaggerated nationalism, and the scorn for democracy and the League of Nations. It is noteworthy that the advent of the dictator states coincided with the new mass communication techniques such as film and radio, which were suited to their needs. But in Italy, due principally to the different temperaments of the two peoples, the best use was not made of all the modern media of persuasion.

During the first decade of Fascist power, from 1922 to about 1933, the various forms of propaganda were not coordinated; nor was there anything like the Nazi Ministry of Propaganda. At the outset films, radio, and all the more modern media were lumped together under Mussolini's press office. Mussolini had been a journalist before he entered politics, and right up to the end of the Fascist era the press was still regarded as the most effective way of influencing public opinion. The Duce referred to it as "an orchestra played in concert, though on different kinds of instruments." By the Press Decree of 1924, prefects were empowered to confiscate issues of newspapers which contained "false information, calculated to inspire class hatred, or to bring the government into contempt." The liberal-minded editors of great newspapers like the *Corriere della Sera* of Milan, or *Il Messaggero* of Rome, were dismissed, and the papers ceased all criticism of the regime. Meanwhile Fascist journals such as Mussolini's *Popolo d'Italia* and the *Regime Fascista* were granted additional subsidies and government aid. By 1926, every paper in Italy had to obtain government permission to publish.

It was not until the 1930s that the regime realized that the press office could not possibly handle all the propaganda media, and in 1933 an Undersecretariat for Press and Propaganda was created. It was not until 1937—after Goebbels' ministry had already been systematically regimenting the German mind for several years—that the German example was followed, and a full-scale Ministry of Propaganda, called the Ministry of Popular Culture (Minculpop), was founded. On June 1 of that year, all the previous offices in the press department—for radio, cinema, theater, literature—were abolished, and those media passed under the control of the new propaganda ministry. From now on, the regime abandoned its purely negative role of censorship, and adopted a more positive approach, issuing directives aimed at indoctrination of Fascist principles in all fields. The ministry was managed by party extremists and had the closest links with the leadership. The three men who followed one another as heads of propaganda, from the undersecretariat days to the ministry, were Count Ciano (Mussolini's son-in-law), Alfieri, and Pavolini. Though their methods became increasingly effective, none of them could be compared with a propaganda genius like Goebbels.

Italy also differed from Germany in the role played by the Catholic church. Because of the church's special position in Italy, and its power over the masses (whether they were devout or not), the regime made no attempt to transform the Fascist doctrines into an alternative religion, as the Nazis had in Germany. The Italian heaven was not to become a Valhalla. This was to have a considerable moderating effect on Fascist policy and propaganda.

In one aspect of propaganda, however, the Fascists always remained the equal of, if not superior to, the Nazis—the indoctrination of the young. Here, the Nazis themselves admitted that in their first years of power they had learned much from Fascist Italy. When Mussolini took office in 1922, he immediately instructed his Education Minister, Giovanni Gentile, to reform the school and university curricula. He understood the importance of youth for the future, and he wanted much more time devoted in the schools to patriotic subjects, with history and geography interpreted in terms of the Roman past. Very soon, at least 20 percent of the curriculum in the elementary schools had been revised in this sense, teaching the adolescent from very early days his duties as a Fascist citizen.

The school day started with the singing of *"Giovinezza"* ("Youth"), the official Fascist hymn. Before beginning their

The Fascist government wanted to teach schoolchildren the qualities of obedience, sacrifice, and intense devotion to the Duce. Mussolini was shown in schoolbooks as a stern but kindly father figure. The text for beginning readers says "Benito Mussolini loves children very much. The children of Italy love the Duce very much. Long live the Duce. I salute the Duce: To us!"

BENITO MUSSOLINI
ama molto i bambini.
I bimbi d'Italia amano
molto il Duce.

VIVA IL DUCE!

Saluto al Duce:

A noi!

Even the comic strips in the youth newspapers were used to instill the virtues of a military caste. (Top) Grillo, from the pages of Il Corriere dei Piccoli, *was already building airplanes in 1934. (Middle) As soon as war was declared in 1940, Romolino and Remoletto were helping the Italian army to fight the British. (Bottom) "Il Balilla Moschettino" (The Balilla Youth "Little Rifle") appeared in the boys' paper* Mastro Remo.

studies, the boys and girls would march past the national flag, giving the ceremonial Roman salute. For the older ones, a series of "Conversations on Fascist Culture" were arranged, conducted by party officials and youth leaders, with subjects such as the History of the Fascist Revolution, Imperialism and Italian Foreign Policy, and the Economic Institutions of Fascism. In higher education at the universities, *Gruppi Universitari Fascisti* were formed, which students had to join if they wished to succeed. At Perugia University, a faculty of political sciences was founded to develop Fascism on doctrinal lines; and a summer school was opened to spread Fascist ideas among foreign students. For the intellectual and professional classes, the Instituto Nazionale Fascista di Cultura was founded by Giovanni Gentile in 1925; its function was to recruit the educated classes into the service of the regime. It had chapters throughout the country and a membership of 100,000. As well as sponsoring lectures and publishing Fascist political theory, the Institute conducted seminars and maintained reading rooms. Similar to this was the Italian Academy, founded in 1927, as "the organ of the Fascist Revolution in the field of Art." But owing to its repressive and stifling atmosphere, it exerted little influence. The regime did, however, succeed in enlisting the support of a few cultural luminaries— Giacomo Puccini, who was rewarded with a seat in the Senate; D'Annunzio, who was given a fine property above the lake of Garda; Luigi Pirandello, and Guglielmo Marconi. Benedetto Croce, Italy's leading intellectual, always remained aloof. Arturo Toscanini was a Fascist in the early days, but when he refused to include the *"Giovinezza"* in his programs he was beaten up by thugs. He resigned from the party, moved permanently to the United States, and refused to conduct in Italy for the duration of the Fascist regime.

Meanwhile in the schools and universities, all the textbooks had been revised; of 317 history books in use in the elementary schools in 1926, 100 were banned. A government decree stated, "In the fields of history, economics and law, all books must be in accord with the historical, juridical and economic requirements established on October 28, 1922." Teachers were required to take an oath of loyalty to the regime, or risk dismissal.

Concurrently with these educational reforms went the creation of the various extramural youth organizations. The Fascists took possesion of the child even earlier than the Nazis did. At the age of four the young boy had to enlist in the "Sons of the She-Wolf," another significant Roman allusion, and don his little black shirt. At eight he graduated into the *Balilla*, where he remained until the age of fourteen, in a continuous atmosphere of uniforms, songs, banners, badges, salutes. (The *Balilla* was named after a Genovese youth who, in 1746, had given the signal for the uprising against the Austrian overlords.)

Children's magazines such as *Il Corriere dei Piccoli* or *Giornale dei Balilla* give some idea of the indoctrination the child underwent. In their comic strips the young hero, aged anywhere between four and ten, wearing a uniform, was depicted instructing other admiring non-*Balilla* children in various sporting activities—yachting, riding, hunting—as well as learning about airplanes, and even how to fire a machine gun. Later, when war came in 1940, the comic strips derided Italy's enemies. Thus, George VI of England and Winston Churchill were shown as being so terrified of the heroic Italian soldiers that they were reduced to hiring an orangutang to protect themselves.

The instruction given in the *Balilla* after school hours and on weekends was essentially physical. The Fascists were well aware of the fascination of sports for the growing boy—football, athletics, swimming, boxing, riding, miniature-range shooting; no expense was spared to provide facilities for these. The Duce set the example himself. He gloried in his own physical fitness, and described boxing as a typically Fascist method of self-expression. Passages were read in school from journalists who had visited him at the Villa Torlonia describing how, while dictating his orders for the day, he would suddenly break off to swim six lengths in his pool, or play a violent set of tennis, or ride his horse over a dozen fences in the paddock. The newspapers were strictly forbidden from reporting that he had a cold or stomach cramps; nor even that he had become a grandfather. The Duce must be 100 percent fit; 100 percent virile.

After the *Balilla* the youth, aged fourteen, joined the *Avant-guardisti*, where to these sports were added sham battles and marching in formation with rifles. He lived in a permanent round of political indoctrination sessions, rallies, military parades, drills, and athletic events. At eighteen he was ready for the *Giovani Fascisti* which, after two more years, would judge whether he was a suitable candidate for the party—whether he was imbued with the necessary virtues of toughness, obedience, blind courage, and self-sacrifice. If so, he was eligible to become a member of the new ruling class of Italy. Each of the graduation ceremonies, from one group to the higher one, was accompanied by an elaborate ritual, the *Leva Fascista*, again recalling ancient Rome.

During the whole indoctrination, the youth were kept constantly aware of the personality of the Duce. His portrait hung in every school and lecture room, beside smaller ones of the king and the pope. With his jaw thrust out, his fists clenched, his arms akimbo and legs apart, he seemed the living image of his own slogans: "Better to live one day like a lion than a hundred years as a sheep"; "A minute on the battlefield is worth a lifetime of peace"; *"Credere! Obbedire! Combattere!"* (Believe! Obey! Fight!")

Thus a boy who started in 1923 as a Son of the She-Wolf would, by the outbreak of war in 1940, have passed through the whole gamut of Fascist education, at four levels. It would take an exceptionally refractory youth to withstand all these impulsions and blandishments.

Parallel youth groups were organized for girls. The *Piccole Italiane* was their counterpart of the Sons of the She-Wolf. Then came the female *Balilla*, with final graduation into the *Giovani Italiane*. Under the auspices of the *Fasci Femminili*, for adults, a set of lectures propagating Fascist principles for women was

(Below) Mussolini, with his bombastic rhetoric, spread before his countrymen the splendor of Imperial Rome. He promised them a share in the Axis hegemony of the Western world. After the decadence of the Second Rome, he heralded the arrival of the Third Rome in which Mussolini himself would perpetuate the glorious ruling tradition of the Caesars. Jack Oakie as Napaloni in Chaplin's The Great Dictator *(1940) portrayed the Duce as a buffoon who played second fiddle to Hitler while Rome burned.*

(Below) Paul Muni as "Scarface" Carmante in Howard Hawks' Scarface: The Shame of a Nation (1932). The film was banned in Rome because it portrayed Italians as gangsters. (Opposite, top) Mussolini was a master of theatrics and overblown oratory. He spoke barechested to show his machismo. (Opposite, bottom) The film industry was not as tightly controlled in Italy as it was in Germany, where Goebbels had the aspirations of a Cecil B. De Mille. L'Uomo del Croce (The Man of the Cross, 1940) was one of the more overtly propagandistic films of the Fascist period. The central character was an Italian priest on the Russian front who took up arms against the Soviets.

given regularly. The older girls were also required to take part in physical training, athletics, even in paramilitary exercises. It was here—and over youth education in general—that the Fascists had their only real dispute with the Catholic church.

The church had always regarded the education of youth as its own special preserve. Pope Pius XI in his encyclical *Non abbiamo bisogno* of 1926 showed that he was fully aware of Fascist pretensions in this area. He wrote: "The undoubted resolve to monopolize completely the young, from their tenderest years up to manhood and womanhood, for the full and exclusive advantages of a party or regime is no less in full conflict with the natural rights of the family than with the supernatural rights of the church." In the view of the Catholic church, youth should be educated by three "societies": the family, the church, and lastly the state. First comes the family, which has a natural God-given right to bring up its offspring, to nourish it, love it, and teach it the elements of civic behavior. Should the family not have the financial means to do this, the state must step in—but only to help. The church possesses all the means for the eternal salvation of the human being. The education, therefore, of that human being, which means the inculcation of moral as well as intellectual values, is the responsibility of the church.

Matters came to a head on May 4, 1928, when a mammoth demonstration took place in the Roman Stadium, where thousands of *Balilla* girls clad in gym clothes gave a physical-training display, and hurled javelins. They then marched in ranks through Rome with rifles at arms-length, chanting Fascist slogans. On May 11, the *Osservatore Romano*, the Vatican newspaper, expressed the Vatican's disapproval of "these groups of Fascist womanhood departing from the principle of modesty and reserve which should govern the education of girls and young women." It was not in keeping with Christian ideals of feminine education for girls, the paper said, to be taught violent physical exercises and to carry firearms; nor for scantily dressed young women to disport themselves in front of predominantly male audiences; nor "to raise their rifles to heaven." "When female hands are raised to heaven," said the pope in a public allocution, "they should be in prayer, not holding rifles."

To this the secretary of the Fascist party, Turati, replied in *Il Tevere* that physical exercise had a beneficial effect on the mind. It was better for young girls to take part in such displays than to spend the day covering their faces with makeup. As for rifles, the regime had no intention of turning the girls into auxiliary troops; it merely wanted to train them not to faint at the sight of a loaded weapon, or when they heard a shot fired in war. The *Osservatore Romano* replied that the girls could perfectly well undergo physical training in the privacy of their school. The paper recalled a speech by Mussolini on May 18, 1927, in which he said he wanted the modern female youth of Italy to remain essentially "Latin," and not allow themselves, "under the influence of the cinema and other forms of modernism, to become Americanized." Well, said the *Osservatore Romano*, that was

(Below) "Keep quiet, the enemy is listening." The British Tommy, used to personify the enemy on this 1943 poster by Gino Boccasile, cocks an ear to pick up military secrets. One of the most common home-front propaganda themes of the war was the threat of "fifth column" activity. Posters linked casual remarks to the sinking of ships and the derailing of trains. Different countries had their own variants of the "careless talk" theme. The British, using puns and cartoons, took a lighter approach. German posters had a cloak-and-dagger quality. To Americans, the connection was often made between a careless comment and its consequences.

IL NEMICO VI ASCOLTA

TACETE!

precisely what the government was doing with these immodest public displays. The notion of females taking part in sporting competitions was essentially Anglo-Saxon. The argument rumbled on for months. It is some measure of the church's power in Italy that the Vatican continued to speak up in this way—to an absolutist regime which had stifled every other voice of criticism. Finally, as a concession to Catholic sensibilities, the Fascists agreed that in the future the girls would not carry rifles at these ceremonies, but bows and arrows.

The Catholic church showed its teeth again on another occasion, in 1928, when the *Balilla* youth introduced a political note into an open-air mass which was being celebrated in the Campo Dux. They began it with the singing of the "*Giovinezza*," followed by an invocation to the Divine Being to help Mussolini in his empire building. Worst of all, when the host was elevated, 15,000 youths drew their daggers from the scabbards and pointed them dramatically to the sky. This was severely reprehended in the *Osservatore Romano*.

These propaganda attempts by the regime to give the impression that the church was on its side were often clumsy. Once, when commemorating the dead Fascist heroes, it evidently thought the church would be flattered by the use of hagiographic language. It described an exhibition of the "Fascist Revolution" as "Fascism's Holy Year," and referred to "the blood of our martyrs, which will one day liquify as does that of Saint Januarius in Naples." A Fascist newspaper in the Trento region wrote of the Italian irredentists, Battisti and Sanro, who had been executed by the Austrians, "There is a halo round the brow of Battisti, whose journey through Trento on the hangman's wagon recalls the journey to Golgotha of the flagellated Christ"; while Sanro's mother "wept before her son's body as did Mary under the Cross." The fertile imagination of one journalist became almost evangelical over a Fascist who had been murdered by communists. "His martyrdom was perhaps greater than that of the blond Nazarene, for the Nazarene was accompanied to his execution by his mother and Mary Magdalene; but our man had no one to support him." The *Osservatore Romano* commented tartly on all this that such attempts to glorify earthly things had in fact the reverse effect. To bring godly and human things together in this way did not of course damage the godly; it only rendered the wordly ridiculous.

The use of recreation and sport as vehicles for propaganda was not confined to the youth of Fascist Italy. To monopolize the leisure time of the working classes on behalf of the regime, an organization entitled *Dopolavoro* ("after working hours") was formed. It offered many attractive and free services and facilities. Besides sport, it provided inexpensive vacations and excursions—as did the *Kraft durch Freude* organization in Nazi Germany—and also films and theatrical performances. Sporting contests among its members were often elaborate spectacles, and the victorious athletes were given personal publicity as examples of the new regime's manliness. *Dopolavoro* was also careful to give lectures and instruction on the party organization, the Fascist Revolution and the Fascist syndicates (trade unions). Its avowed purpose was "the healthy and profitable occupation of workers' leisure hours through institutions for developing their physical, intellectual, and moral capacities."

To outlying provinces, the party sent mobile theater groups to present Fascist morality plays, usually followed by political commentaries from local party leaders. In Milan, the brashness of the leadership was revealed in a set of lectures it arranged called *Lectura Ducis*, modeled on the *Lectura Dantis*, a famous set of lectures on Dante Alighieri given by renowned scholars in the Florentine church of Orsanmichele. In the series *Lectura Ducis* a party leader read from Mussolini's speeches, and then commented on them in Dantesque phraseology. The Duce was to be not only the new Caesar but, in political thought, the new Dante as well.

As a propaganda vehicle, the cinema was never exploited as extensively in Italy as in Nazi Germany. Up to the end of the Fascist era, the Italian film companies still remained largely in private hands. This was due primarily to the Italian public's lack of interest in serious films about politics, such as the government-made *Battle of the Grain*, incorporating shots of Mussolini driving about on a tractor surrounded by vociferating peasants. The public preferred American-type films about glamorous couples eating caviar in chic hotels, or driving Cadillacs. Deplorable as this was, the regime knew there was not much to be done about it. When in the thirties someone suggested to Mussolini that he should take a leaf out of Goebbels' book and nationalize the film companies, he refused. The attitude of his regime towards the cinema, at least in the first decade of Fascist rule, was that of a censor. The concern was with what could *not* be shown, rather than what should be shown. Thus, a "decadent" Hollywood film such as *Wings over Honolulu* was banned, because it dealt with the immoral goings-on of a group of divorcees. Although this ban may have been in part to ingratiate the church, divorce conflicted with Fascist principles about the sanctity of marriage and the rearing of large families. The film *Scarface* was banned for other reasons. It was about gangster life in Chicago, and its protagonist was the Sicilian mobster Al Capone; it might give wrong ideas to his countrymen at home.

In spite of this, Mussolini knew perfectly well that the cinema had propaganda value. In 1925, he founded *L'Unione Cinematografica Educativa* (LUCE), a purely governmental body which produced documentaries about Fascist achievements. To counteract the influence of the American-type "high life" film, all cinemas were required to include at least one LUCE film in every program. Thus, if the public wanted to watch Cary Grant making love to Mae West, they also had to look at an old peasant in the Pontine Marshes, on the horns of a dilemma about whether he should adopt modern farming methods or remain true to those of his fathers. This was the LUCE film *Il Sole* (*The Sun*). Another LUCE film, *I ragazzi di Mussolini* (*Mussolini's Youth*), showed what the Duce was doing for the youth of Italy.

(Below) "To the army, to the army, youth of Italy, for the salvation of the country." This recruiting poster was one of a series seen on the streets of Rome in late 1943. As Italy's military fortunes declined, the "New Rome" became an extended family; the matriarch replaced the Duce in the appeal for more soldiers. (Following spread) Mussolini's ability to spellbind an audience equaled that of the greatest Italian actors. His use of gesture, voice modulation, and emotional extremes were exceptional. This flamboyance, enshrined in bronze and stone, adorned public plazas throughout Italy.

(Below) The Duce was an easy target
for the mockery of cartoonists abroad.
This 1937 cartoon by the Soviet artists,
the Kukriniksi, lampoons the pretension
of Mussolini's "New Rome," where
vast monuments were erected in the
Foro Mussolini, modeled on the ancient
Roman Forum. The Kukriniksi showed
Mussolini as an oppressive dictator
whose pedestal was a prison.

In the LUCE films, army maneuvers, battleships, and bombing planes were also given a prominent place, which may have made them a little more palatable to the Italian public.

It was not until 1937 that anything to compare with the Nazi film *Triumph of the Will* was produced. It was called *Credere, Obbedire, Combattere* (*Believe, Obey, Fight*), and it showed the achievements of Fascism, accompanied by selected excerpts from Mussolini's speeches. This was followed by other patriotic films, expensive productions such as *Scipio Africanus* (1937), which drew the parallel between ancient Rome's conqueror of Carthage and Mussolini, who had just conquered another part of Africa, Ethiopia. It was made in Rome, and when it was shown the carping Italian critics pointed to the anachronism of telegraph poles sprouting on the hills and wrist watches on the arms of the Roman legionaries.

The Italian invasion of Ethiopia was also the subject of *Luciano Serra Pilota* (1938), about the instinctive passion for flying which passes from father to son. It told of a father who lost his life flying in Ethiopia to save his son. In 1940 came *The Siege of Alcazar*, proudly relating Italy's part in the Spanish Civil War. Later in the Second World War, when things were going badly, a film was made to appeal to Italian nationalist rather than Fascist sentiment: *L'Uomo della Croce* (*The Man of the Cross,* 1943). This was about an Italian priest on the Russian front who exchanges his cross for a rifle, and fights with the black shirts against the Soviets.

Radio as a propaganda instrument was better handled. It could be centrally controlled and made to broadcast the bulletins of the government press agency, Stefani, which alone could dispense news abroad, because it had the monopoly of contracts with all foreign press associations, such as Reuters and Associated Press. Although Mussolini hardly used the radio for studio talks himself, preferring like Hitler the balcony approach, he realized that thanks to this new medium his open-air speeches could be heard all over Italy. His aim was, he proclaimed, "to see a radio in every home." To this end, a cheap set, significantly named the *Balilla*, was put on the market at 430 lire, which was payable in 18 monthly installments. As the figures reveal, it had some success. Whereas in 1927 there were 40,000 subscribers to the *Ente Italiano Audizione Radiofonica,* by 1939 there were 1,170,000. But for a population of 43 million this could hardly compare with the 12,500,000 sets which Germany had in the same year. It was not until 1937 that the Inspectorate for Radio Broadcasting was made part of the Ministry of Popular Culture. From Germany the Fascists borrowed the habit of installing a communal radio set in the halls and recreation rooms where the peasants gathered in the evenings, and where they could listen to government announcements. Loudspeakers were also placed in the piazzas and outside the offices of local authorities.

The Fascists also used the radio extensively in youth education. The program *"Giornalino del Fanciullo"* ("Children's Little Newspaper") broadcast stories, poems, songs, and religious

Project for a standard monument in the Italian " empire."

services, interspersed with tales of fabulous exploits by Mussolini and other Italian heroes. Special attention was also paid to the countryside through the *Ente Radio Rurale*, providing regular agricultural news and advice to the peasantry.

The regime's greatest radio achievement was in support of the invasion of Ethiopia. Just before it began, in October 1935, the Fascist party organized huge assemblies all over Italy, in every town and village, with songs, bands, sirens, and patriotic speeches by fiery local party leaders. Then, when an estimated 20 million people were gathered, the voice of the Duce came announcing that Italy, too, was about to take her "place in the sun." On a thousand piazzas, his booming voice infected the mob with collective hysteria, and they shrieked their approval—just as fifteen years earlier in Fiume, D'Annunzio had worked up the population of a small and modest town to a state of insensate frenzy. After this, the Fascists could claim that these unanimous cries of approval for the Ethiopian invasion were tantamount to a national plebiscite, and that the Duce was only carrying out the people's will.

On May 9, 1936, after the Italian army's triumph in Ethiopia, Mussolini appeared on the balcony of the Palazzo Venezio to announce the foundation of the new Italian Empire under Vittorio Emmanuele III, who would henceforth assume the style and dignity of the king-emperor. Rome had been born again. Radio sets and loudspeakers throughout Italy blared out the Duce's words. "The Italian people," he cried, "have created the empire with their own blood. They will nourish it with their own labor, and defend it against all comers with their own arms. Supremely confident of this, lift up your mansards, my legionaries, your weapons and your hearts, to salute after fifteen centuries, the reappearance of our empire on the fateful hills of Rome! Are you not worthy of it?"

Another form of propaganda during the Fascist period was the holding of immense exhibitions. The greatest of these was the *Mostra della Rivoluzione Fascista* (Exhibition of the Fascist Revolution) in Rome on the tenth anniversary of the seizure of power. Under one large roof were gathered exhibits from the years 1914–22, among which were the bloody uniforms and medals of the martyrs who died during the March on Rome. The exhibition also included a "sacrarium," or votive chapel to the Fascist fallen. The quasireligious atmosphere was further enhanced by the great cross in the center of a semicircle bearing the illuminated words, "*Per la Patria Immortale*" and "*Presente! Presente!*" (that is, our dead are still with us), and "To us! To us!" Millions of country dwellers were attracted to Rome for this exhibition by reduced fares and free excursions organized by the local Fascist authorities.

Posters were created for the Duce by Italy's leading graphic artists. Foremost among them was Gino Boccasile, whose posters epitomized the Fascist themes: the courage of the black shirts against the Allies, anti-Semitism, and the portrayal of the enemy soldiers as barbarians.

The Fascists excelled in the concoction of slogans, surpassing

(Below) Few observers outside Italy were fooled by the propaganda of the Rome-Berlin axis, which Mussolini, in a 1936 speech in Milan, said was "not a diaphragm but an axis, around which can resolve all those European states with a will to collaboration and peace." Abroad, Mussolini's bombast was disregarded and he was portrayed as Hitler's lackey, as in this 1936 Soviet cartoon by Boris Efimov.

(Top) A British "black" parody stamp paraphrased Mussolini's slogan, "Two nations, one war," as "Two nations, one Führer." (Bottom) Like two actors, the Führer and the Duce rode through the streets of Berlin, which were decorated by Germany's outstanding stage designer, Benno von Arendt. (Opposite page, top) Hitler and Mussolini greet crowds in Rome. (Bottom) Art mirrors life in this scene from Chaplin's The Great Dictator.

even the Nazis. Mussolini the ex-journalist knew the power of the written word, and he personally was a great coiner of slogans. They were to be found scrawled on half the walls and wayside buildings of Italy: "He who has steel has bread!"; "War is to the male what childbearing is to the female!"; "All within the State, nothing outside the State, nothing against the State!"; "The Fascist man does not believe in everlasting peace"; "Nothing has been won in history without bloodshed"; "Right without might is vain"; "The plough makes the furrow, but the sword defends it!" And the most famous of all, *"Mussolini ha sempre ragione!"* ("Mussolini is always right!").

An acid comment on this slogan mania was made by Hitler himself on his ceremonial visit to Italy in May, 1938. Albert Speer, who was with him, writes in his memoirs that Hitler was not at all impressed by the walls he saw everywhere daubed with these phrases. *"We* don't need that," he said. "The German people are tough enough, if it comes to war. This kind of propaganda may be all right in Italy. Whether it does any good is another matter." Hitler knew little of foreign countries and peoples, and his comment is of more value about himself, and his overweening conceit, than about the Italian slogans. They were devised by leaders who knew their countrymen.

It was during Hitler's visit that Mussolini fell completely under the spell of his more powerful fellow dictator. He had first met Hitler in Venice in 1934, and had not been impressed by him; of *Mein Kampf* he had said, "that boring book which I have never been able to read." But by 1936, as Hitler consolidated his power and supported Italy's aggression in Ethiopia, Mussolini began to change his opinion. In Milan in that year he referred to the "axis" for Italo-German collaboration. "The Berlin-Rome line is not a diaphragm," he said, "but rather an axis around which can revolve all those European states with a will to collaboration and peace."

On an earlier visit he had made to Germany, in September, 1937, Mussolini had been much impressed by the German army, at whose magnificent parades he had been the guest of honor. It was then that he told Ciano, "We must make the Italians harder, nastier, more hateful, more Prussian." With this in mind, he introduced the German goose step into the Italian army, because "it is strong, secure, inexorable, making every march into a conquest," and is "so difficult that a lazy or weak person cannot perform it." This did not please the Italian king, who was far from pro-German. But Mussolini brushed his criticism aside with the explanation, "The goose is after all a Roman bird. Did it not save the Capitol?" He ordered that the goose step was to be known in the Italian army as *il passo Romano* (the Roman step).

On the Führer's return visit to Italy, Mussolini was determined that it should be as impressive as his own to Germany. Planning began six months before, and Mussolini spent hours supervising the arrangements of the military parades, and checking the details of every march. Particular care was paid to the decoration of the streets, to give Hitler a splendid welcome. Al-

*After Mussolini's visit to Germany in
1937, the Italian army was ordered
to adopt the goose step, renamed the
"passo romano" (Roman step).
Mussolini claimed that it symbolized
the will and energy of youth. The step,
he said, was difficult; lazy and weak
people couldn't do it. Nevertheless,
the Italian soldier was ridiculed as a
coward in such films as Billy Wilder's*
Five Graves to Cairo.

though some of the Roman shopkeepers refused to display Hitler's photograph in their windows, the German dictator was suitably impressed. He felt that even if Italy was not particularly strong militarily, here was an ally he dare not lose.

Much more serious and sinister was the anti-Semitism which Mussolini, again aping his German mentor, introduced into Italy at the end of the thirties. Before 1938, he had emphatically rejected anti-Semitism. Now, after entering into the "Pact of Steel" with Hitler, he made it an official tenet of the regime. There were only about 50,000 Jews in Italy, and anti-Semitism hardly existed. But the dictatorship issued manifestos on the German lines, stating that the Italian race was pure, and that the Jews did not belong to it, however long their families had lived there. Racist magazines such as *La Difensa della Razza* (*The Defense of the Race*) were published. Courses were held on such topics as "Preserving Racial Integrity"; "The Danger of Mixed Marriages"; "The Purity of the Italian Race since Roman Times"; and "The Jews and Modern Culture." These lectures received wide press and radio publicity, and some were published in book form for use in the schools. Decrees were issued forbidding the entry of foreign Jews into schools, and preventing them from settling in Italy. Italians were later forbidden from marrying Jews, and Jews were excluded from the army. But no amount of propaganda could stir up much feeling in a country where there was probably less anti-Semitism than anywhere else in Europe. When the war came, much energy which could have been employed elsewhere had been wasted in this unprofitable field.

Together with the Fascist propaganda to transform Italy into a race of warriors as valiant as the legionaries of ancient Rome went a campaign to represent her enemies as unmilitary and decadent. By the late thirties, Mussolini had become convinced that the main opponent to his expansionist plans would be Great Britain. In 1936, Britain had done everything short of war to impede his invasion of Ethiopia, sponsoring the League of Nations' economic sanctions against Italy. The failure of these gave Mussolini the excuse he required for exacerbating Italian nationalism still further. Italy's success in Ethiopia proved, he said, that the British navy's domination of the Mediterranean was over. Gone were the high colonial days when men like Rhodes, Kitchener, and Lord Roberts made the British Empire great. Britain was now governed by a pusillanimous businessman armed with nothing more than an umbrella. Italy would supplant Britain in North Africa and the Mediterranean.

An excerpt from an article in the Fascist magazine *Gerarchia* illustrates the scorn which was being fostered for Great Britain (January 1938): "Englishmen are incapable of understanding great ideas, and they have a profound dislike of anything theoretical or abstract . . . They lack any real intelligence . . . but are moved solely by material ambitions and immediate interests . . . In the pursuit of personal advantage, they assume attitudes which are often contradictory and absurd . . . Their's is a country without literature and without art or music . . . Serious scholarship is derided in England and intellectual subjects are never discussed . . . Only the sheer ignorance of John Bull and the docile attitude of official writers could ever have suggested that such a chaotic agglomeration as the British Empire could resemble the empire of ancient Rome . . ."

In addition to journalists, eminent professors of biology and anthropology were enlisted to show that the Anglo-Saxon race was effete and degenerate. In the years immediately before the Second World War, the Fascists created an image of an Anglo-Saxon society based entirely on wealth—or "gold," as they preferred to call it. Their slogans referred to the coming struggle between gold (the bourgeois democracies) and work (the "proletarian" axis nations). The Western plutocracies, they asserted, could maintain their domination in the world only by gold, for in all other spheres they were inferior. With gold, however, they intended to strangle the new, young, and vigorous societies surging in Italy and Germany, whose strength lay not in gold but in work. The Duce was "the creator of the civilization of work." When the struggle came, victory would go to the work nations, for work was the highest, noblest, most spiritual expression of life.

All this anti-British propaganda the Italian public was forced to swallow in increasing quantities as the international tensions grew. The journalist Ermanno Amicucci went so far as to say, "Thanks to the heroism of our soldiers, gold will prove incapable of subjugating work—in a holy war against the slavemaster, gold, and the ferocious egotism of our hereditary enemy, the British Empire, the profiteer for centuries of the blood and sweat of others . . ." The British were accused of every form of vice and foppery. Their energy, it was said, was sapped not only by their worship of Mammon, but by such crankish addictions as psychonalysis and spiritualism, five-o'clock tea, golf (the "anti-Mediterranean sport"), even by the unmasculine habit of shaving once a day. The Italian public was told that in English secondary schools, young girls were bought and sold, their principal purchasers being Anglican bishops and members of Parliament. The historian Alessandro Luzzio said that the English were a race of drunkards, drug addicts, and homosexuals, being encouraged in the latter vice by "the many thickets conveniently placed in Hyde Park," and by the ugliness of English women. There were seven million spinsters in England, whose sexual frustration could be relieved only by a royal decree permitting polygamy.

As for the British fighting qualities, their army was composed largely of Indian mercenaries and Australian ex-convicts; it would mutiny rather than parade in the rain, and it always broke off action at five o'clock for tea. Even the usually well-informed Italian ambassador in London, Count Grandi, subscribed to this rubbish. He informed his government that the British Brigade of Guards could not stand up for a moment to their Italian counterparts. The British were, he said, "a people entirely without the military virtues."

It might appear from all this that the Fascist propagandists

(Below) The text of Boccasile's poster reads "Germany is your friend." In 1940 Mussolini said, "If the Germans ever get here they will never go home." Immediately after Mussolini's fall in 1943, Hitler sent German troops to Italy to occupy the country. After a bitter struggle, the Germans were defeated in May 1945 by the Allies, whom the disillusioned and weary Italians welcomed as liberators.

(Bottom) The Kukriniksi, who had earlier drawn Hitler goose-stepping in an Italian boot, now showed him trying to extricate his foot from that same boot. Actually, Hitler was prepared to fight to the end. In January 1944, German troops established the Gustav Line to defend Rome, which Hitler said "must be held at all costs for the sake of the political consequences which would follow a completely successful defense." This was another tactical error which ended in defeat.

had gone off their heads, and that their charges were not worthy of rebuttal. But these are only a few of the accusations about British decadence which are listed, in all seriousness, by the eminent British historian and expert on Fascist Italy, Professor Dennis Mack Smith, in his study of anti-British propaganda, *Inghilterra e Italia nel' 900.*

Great Britain's potential allies, France and later the United States, came in for a similar, if less virulent, treatment. France with her popular front government was, the Fascists deduced, clearly under the domination of a foreign power, the Soviets, and therefore not fit to call herself a sovereign state. She too was corrupted by innumerable modern vices—contraception and the low birth rate, gambling, the immoral writings of Marcel Proust and André Gide, Pernod, bathing shorts, permanent waves. France would collapse like a pack of cards at the first cannonade. Nor was she fit to administer North African territories like Tunisia which was, in any case, "an Italian province governed by French bureaucrats."

The United States did not come in for this sort of abuse until the spring of 1940, when her sympathies were clearly veering towards the Western Allies. Short-wave broadcasts from Radio Roma were now addressed to the large Italian community in the United States, fostering an isolationist feeling. The broadcasts condemned President Roosevelt for plotting to involve his country in a war which could bring only suffering and disaster to all Americans.

This sort of propaganda was relatively successful in peacetime when the Anglo-Saxon powers, busy with their commercial affairs, could not be bothered to counter it. But in war, when they revealed that they could not only defend themselves but could go on the offensive with an avalanche of ad hoc armaments, the decadence propaganda began to ring hollow. The Italians are more cynical than the Germans, and they had no Goebbels to make up their minds for them. In the first weeks after the Italian entry into the war, the Italian newspapers made ludicrous claims, announcing that Italy now had complete mastery of the Mediterranean. In three days, they said, the Italian air force had sunk half the British fleet; it was now turning its attention to the Battle of Britain and destroying the RAF in its own skies. The first claim was quickly disposed of by the Battle of Cape Matapan, where the British navy gave the Italian fleet such a mauling that it hardly dared show its nose again outside territorial waters for the rest of the war. Fascist claims about the Battle of Britain and their part in the bombing of London were soon seen to be equally absurd. *Il Tempo* wrote on January 16, 1941, "The city of London, the citadel of British commerce, is burning down. Soon the whole of England will burn down to its last house, its last tree, its last man." The verb *coventrizzare* —derived from the city of Coventry, whose cathedral had been destroyed by German bombs—was delightedly coined to describe the nemesis which would shortly overtake all the cities of Great Britain. Nevertheless, all this ruin did not appear to affect the RAF, which began visiting the cities of northern Italy nightly, peppering them with high explosives in ever increasing quantities.

The finest propaganda in the world cannot make up for military defeats. Probably Hitler's greatest propaganda mistake was, in a moment of euphoria in late 1941, to announce that the Soviet Union had been beaten and the war won. Even Goebbels could not afterwards fully repair the damage done to the public mind. In the same way, as the Italian defeats multiplied and the Italian army was ejected by the "decadent" British and American troops from one place after another, and the African empire crumbled before the people's eyes, they began to lose faith in the words of their leaders. Just as Mussolini had, as the war continued, announced his increasing belief in the German alliance, so the Italian people began to withdraw theirs. They began to hate the Germans more than the Allies.

Here, Allied propaganda in the form of pamphlets from the air proved particularly effective. The British had the brilliant idea of invoking the sacred name of Garibaldi in their pamphlets. Garibaldi had once said in a famous speech that Italy's future after unification would remain always linked with England's. The pamphlets read:

THE CURSE OF GARIBALDI!

Giuseppe Garibaldi, whose name is revered wherever free men live, said in 1854, "Should England ever call for help to an ally, cursed be that Italian who fails to answer the call!" Benito Mussolini, by leading you under the yoke of your secular enemy, the Teuton, has brought down that curse upon you!

THE CURSE OF GARIBALDI HAS COME HOME TO ROOST!

Benito Mussolini, obedient to the commands of Hitler, informed you that the defeat of France signified the defeat of England. But Hitler has not defeated England. He therefore brought you into the war on his side, so that the English bombs destined for Germany might rain down on you!

THE CURSE OF GARIBALDI IS NOW COMING TO YOU IN THE FORM OF BOMBS!

To this the Italian propagandists retaliated with posters depicting a far greater curse than bombs which would descend on Italy if the Anglo-Saxons won the war—barbarism. Their propaganda about barbarian mercenaries in the British army was supplemented when the United States came into the war by Boccasile's famous poster of an American black G.I. carrying off the marble statue of the Venus de Milo with a $2 price ticket attached to its neck. The Americans would plunder and destroy the cultural treasures of the more civilized continent. Another poster depicted a brutalized British Tommy leering out from under a tin hat. The well-known Italian "mamma" cult was exploited in a sentimental poster of an elderly peasant woman of great dignity, in bombazine black, proudly wearing on her bosom the medal for gallantry won by her son, who was killed in action. "Do not betray my son!" she solemnly warns.

A caricature of Mussolini by the Brazilian artist José Ozon, 1944. The Duce had already fallen from power. Before his death at the hands of Italian partisans he was propped up by the Germans as a puppet ruler in northern Italy. The wind had gone out of his sails and he remained only the shell of his former self.

(Below) The Kukriniksi in this 1943 caricature caught the essence of the sagging dictator who was ousted from power in July 1943. Mussolini told a friend a few months later that the Italian people hated him as much in defeat as they had loved him in victory. Though one Fascist committed suicide when he heard of Mussolini's removal, it generally caused little stir other than a sense of relief; not a single voice was raised in his defense.

For propaganda to the United States, the Fascists employed the American auricular poet Ezra Pound, an admirer of Mussolini and a rabid anti-Semite. He broadcast twice weekly from Radio Roma via short wave to the United States, and also wrote scripts in English for Italian propagandists. Sometimes he attacked President Roosevelt as a "warmonger"; sometimes, when he was for some curious reason announced as "Ezra Pound, the poet and economist," he expatiated on the monetary reforms necessary to save the United States from disaster. Sometimes, he read his own poetry or talked about his literary friends (which caused most of the listeners to switch off). He claimed to be protesting less against present conditions than against "a system which creates one war after another." He remained in Italy ranting against the Allies until the end of the war, when the American army picked him up and indicted him for treason. He was found insane, and confined to a mental institution. He was released after a decent interval, to die in his adopted land, Italy. Of all the propaganda episodes of the Second World War, his was one of the most sordid.

Against Soviet Russia, Fascist propaganda aimed at persuading Italians to fight beside the German Waffen SS on the Eastern front. This worked well enough when the Germans were advancing in the hot summer months; but the first defeats in the Russian snows quickly disillusioned the Italian volunteers. A number of them were also attracted by the good pay in Germany, to go there and work in the Todt Organization which required their technical skill. They too were soon disillusioned when they found that they were treated by their allies as members of an inferior race.

With the fall of Mussolini in the autumn of 1943, Badoglio and a number of other Fascist renegades acted as an interim government. For some months, they attempted to maintain the fiction of a German alliance, and continued to brand the Allies as "barbarian invaders." But the Italian people had had enough; they welcomed the Allies not as barbarians, because that propaganda word had been overdone, but as liberators, and Badoglio was forced to adopt their viewpoint.

In the period of Fascist propaganda examined here, 1922–1945, comparisons between the Fascist and Nazi methods are inevitable, owing to the similar state structures. Although the Fascists were in the propaganda business twice as long—twenty-three years to the Nazis' twelve—it cannot be said that they were as successful. In the field of mob oratory there was probably little to choose, but on the whole the cynical Italians proved harder to delude. Compared with the ominous workings of Dr. Goebbels, Italian propaganda methods proved to be dilettantish, surprisingly ill-informed about other nations, and frequently ludicrous.

Cover of the magazine Fascist Youth, *late 1920s/Italy/A. Canevari.*

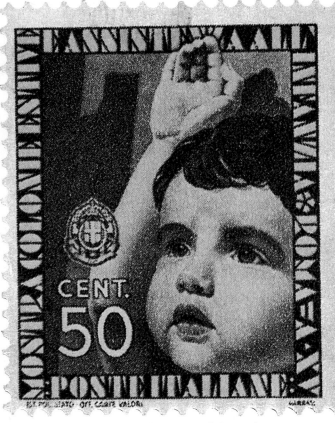

Issued to commemorate the Summer Exhibition for Child Welfare, June 28, 1937/Italy/Artist unknown.

(Top and bottom, left) More Child Welfare commemoratives. (Bottom, right) Fascist Legionary issue on the founding of Italian East Africa, 1938/ Italy/Artist unknown.

Allied "black" parody of Italian stamp,
c. 1944/Allied propaganda for Italy/
Artist unknown.

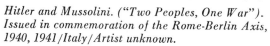

Hitler and Mussolini. ("Two Peoples, One War").
Issued in commemoration of the Rome-Berlin Axis,
1940, 1941/Italy/Artist unknown.

*"Enlist in the Auxiliary Service of the
X Flotilla MAS," no date/Italy/Artist unknown.*

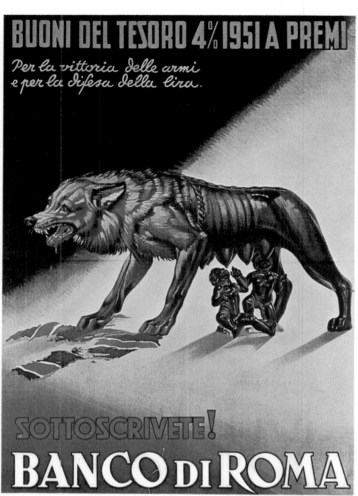

"No march on Moscow without the March on
Rome," 1942/Italy/Alberto Amorico.

"Buy Treasury Bonds from the Bank of Rome,"
1942/Italy/A. Capitani.

"All and everyone for victory," 1941/Italy/
Artist unknown.

"Enlist in the Italian SS Legion," c. 1943/
Italy/Gino Boccasile.

Anti-British postcards, c. 1941/
Italy/A. Bertiglia.

NOTIZIE DA ROMA
VE LE MANDA LA FEDERAZIONE FASCISTA DELL'URBE

Roma · Anno VIII · 22 Novembre XX · N. 56 · Settimanale edito dalla Federazione dell'Urbe

Non è soltanto con l'oro che si vincono le guerre. Oltre all'oro è più importante la volontà e ancora più importante il coraggio.

Mussolini

SPAZIO VITALE

L'unità economica, l'omogeneità politica, la collaborazione spirituale e sociale europee che l'Inghilterra era sempre riuscita ad impedire, con la marcia vittoriosa dell'Asse diventano di giorno in giorno realtà splendente. Alle porte dell'Europa, verso l'Asia, si sta costituendo un immenso spazio destinato a servire come territorio di colonizzazione, di investimenti, di produzione per le eccedenze demografiche ed economiche continentali.

Per tale spazio, ricchissimo di risorse minerarie, agricole, zoologiche, forestali la nuova Europa si renderà del tutto indipendente nei confronti degli altri continenti. E l'America del Nord, che attraverso il bolscevismo e l'aiuto interessato prestato all'Inghilterra voleva appropriarsi di queste ricchezze costringendo alla fame e alla servitù tutti i popoli della Europa, sarà la prima a scontare la nuova situazione di fatto creata dalla illuminata volontà dei due Condottieri, il Duce e il Fuehrer, dall'eroismo dei popoli italiano e germanico e loro alleati.

Qual'è quel Paese..?

Qual'è quel Paese dove la base della Nazione non è la famiglia, ma... il divorzio?

Gli Stati Uniti d'America.

Dove è in uso la rapina e l'uccisione dei bambini a scopo di ricatto?

Gli Stati Uniti d'America.

Dove l'alcoolismo è una... istituzione?

Dove lo Stato non è nelle mani del Capo, ma della di lui moglie?

Dove la Presidentessa fa la sguattera dell'ebraismo imperante e il Presidente il ragazzo dell'ascensore...?

Dove la polizia fa a mezzo con i gangsters? Dove si sovvenziona il comunismo russo, la barbarie tartara, la delinquenza serba - facendo in questo concorrenza all'Inghilterra - per rendere schiavi i popoli del lavoro, del genio e dell'arte, i veri « civilizzatori », e cioè l'italiano, il germanico e il giapponese? Dove la fame di oro e di lusso è tale che non basta più il continente americano e si vuole impadronirsi dell'Europa, dell'Asia e dell'Africa? Dove si vuol dichiarare la guerra alla... Finlandia? Dove si ignorano la storia, la luce, la verità di Roma?

Gli Stati Uniti, sempre gli Stati Uniti.

E questa gente vorrebbe dettar legge proprio a noi.

Ma la storia non è fatta dai gangsters, nè da Giuda, nè dalla coppia Roosevelt, nè da Churchill, da Stalin ecc.: è fatta dai popoli che credono nella giustizia di Dio e nel Suo nome combattono.

I convogli di Roosevelt verso la tragica meta

Certe benedizioni

Durante un banchetto di 37 portate - che razza di comunismo! - Stalin ha invocato la benedizione di Dio sul capo di Roosevelt.

Dio pronunciato dalla bocca di Stalin?

Questi sono scherzi del diavolo.

No, non lo faranno

Stalin è furibondo: lo fanno o no gli inglesi lo sbarco sul Continente europeo?

E' proprio rimbambito questo svaligiatore di diligenze: non sa ancora che gli inglesi sono specialisti in "reimbarchi,,.

Roma · Anno VIII · 22 Novembre XX · N. 56 · Settimanale edito dalla Federazione dell'Urbe   STABILIMENTO TIPOGRAFICO DELLA U.E.S.I.S.A.   SISTO FAVRE   Spedizione in abbonamento postale · Manifesto del Partito Nazionale Fascista · Esente da bollo   EDITRICE DE « IL LAVORO FASCISTA » · ROMA

Anti-American poster with the theme of 'cultural barbarism,' c. 1942/Italy/Gino Boccasile.

*Anti-Semitic poster portraying the stereotyped
Jewish Bolshevik, c. 1942/Italy/Gino Boccasile.*

"Workers, rebuild the country," 1943/Italy/
Artist unknown.

"Good blood doesn't lie," 1944/Italy/
Artist unknown.

"*Italian workers, enlist for Germany,*" 1943/
German poster for Italy/Artist unknown.

"*The spirit of Goffredo Mameli will defend
the Republic,*" 1944/Italy/Artist unknown.

"Bread and welfare. See the Todt Organization,"
1944/German poster for Italy/Artist unknown.

"The fate of the saboteur," 1944/Italy/
Artist unknown.

*"Kick out the Germans," 1943/OWI poster for
Italy/Artist unknown.*

The work of the "liberators," 1944/Italy/
Artist unknown.

Lavoratori d'Italia!
I "Liberatori" già da oggi pensano
per l'avvenire dei vostri figli...

*"Italian workers! Here's how the 'liberators' will treat
your children," c. 1944/Italy/Artist unknown.*

BRITAIN IMPROVISES
1936-1945

When the Axis powers set such store
by organization, the British applied
improvisation to good effect.
HAROLD LASWELL

Great Britain emerged from World War I with the doubtful distinction of having employed propaganda better than any other nation. This was largely due to one man, Alfred Harmsworth, later Lord Northcliffe, father of the yellow press. When the war was going badly in 1917, he persuaded Prime Minister Lloyd George and the cabinet that skillful denigration of the Germans could stimulate the flagging energies of the British people. Lloyd George let him establish a propaganda department in Crewe House. Within a year, thanks to his powerful newspaper conglomerate, Northcliffe had convinced most of his countrymen that the Germans were ruthless savages, violators of women, and inventors of the "*kadaver* factory," a chemical process by which soldiers' corpses could be converted into fats for the manufacture of explosives.

This was all primarily for home consumption. For the enemy, Northcliffe put into practice advice he had often vouchsafed, unheeded, to the General Staff—"The bombardment of the enemy mind is almost as important as his bombardment by guns." In the last year of the war, millions of leaflets composed by Crewe House—four million in August 1918 alone—were delivered across the German lines by balloon or shot over in shells. They informed the Germans of their hopeless plight, of the grand coalition now against them, with legions of completely fresh American troops, and of the hunger and starvation which awaited them as a result of the Allied blockade if they did not give in. On another level, the leaflets appealed to the large Social Democratic element still vocal in Germany, which had long admired British democratic institutions. The leaflet propaganda suggested that if the Germans would only expel their autocratic rulers, a new "liberal" Germany which the Allies would foster could be developed on Westminster lines.

But promises have to be kept. As soon as the war was over, Lord Northcliffe's department was closed, and his little group of propagandists went back to their respectable peacetime pursuits—zoology, law, teaching, and the like. No more was heard of them in Germany. The German Social Democrats complained that they had been duped by this Allied propaganda. They had done exactly what they were told—booted out the Kaiser and replaced him with a former saddler, Friedrich Ebert, as head of state. But the Allies, ran the Germans' reasoning, instead of supporting the new Weimar Republic, had done all they could to discountenance it—exorbitant reparations demands, the Versailles "war guilt" clause, and the occupation of the Rhineland by French and African troops.

Northcliffe's propaganda had a boomerang effect in another way. He was unwise enough after the war to boast publicly of what his discreditable methods had achieved. When the "German atrocities" were found to be grossly exaggerated, if not fictitious, the word propaganda became anathema for those in England who had believed them.

This disillusionment was largely responsible for the abandonment of propaganda as a government activity in England when the war ended. In any case the British, who had for cen-

(Top) Sir Oswald Mosley was the demagogic leader of the British Union of Fascists, though his public-school background added a polished tone to his conviction. After 1938, Mosley's party was torn by dissension and declined rapidly. (Bottom) Trade Unionists and Laborites came out early against the Nazis, as this 1934 poster indicates. The Peace Movement was strong in England before Germany declared war.

NATIONAL JOINT COUNCIL
Representing
The Trades Union Congress
The Labour Party   and
The Parliamentary Labour Party

DEUTSCHLAND

MADE IN GERMANY

NO MORE WAR !
NO MORE WAR PROFITEERING !!
REFUSE GERMAN GOODS !!!

National Joint Council, Transport House, Smith Square, London

turies dominated half the globe, did not believe it was necessary in peacetime to advertise themselves or decry their adversaries. Northcliffe's activities were "not cricket." Nevertheless by the 1930s, British diplomatic missions in such sensitive areas as the Middle East and Latin America were becoming increasingly alarmed at the damage being done to British interests by well-directed propaganda from Italy, Germany, and the Soviet Union through government-controled press agencies, radio stations, and cultural organizations. In 1934, the British government responded to their missions' demands for something to counter this propaganda—though on a modest scale. The government established the British Council, whose charter defined its aim as "the promotion of a wider knowledge of Britain and the English language abroad, and the development of closer cultural relations between Britain and other countries." But so meager was the council's allowance that it could do little more than distribute brochures and photographs about cherished British institutions —the Horse Guards and Trooping the Color, Oxford and Cambridge, Ascot, the green sward of the Cathedral closes, and so on.

Meanwhile, the declamatory propaganda used at home in the late 1930s by the British branch of the Fascist Party under Sir Oswald Mosley did not attract the British public, which despised Mosley's demagogic methods and noisy blackshirt followers.

Yet even before Hitler came to power, there were a few men, who, having seen what propaganda had done in World War I, had been warning the government that an organized information service would be as necessary as any other line of defense in a future war. At the time of Munich in 1938 and the appeasement policy of Neville Chamberlain—which had a considerable popular following—these men, like Winston Churchill and Duff Cooper, saw the danger ahead. It was not until 1938 that government funds were made available for a foreign service of the BBC, which broadcast news, cultural talks, and English language instruction to Europe, South America, and the Middle East.

At the outbreak of war in 1939, two more propaganda bodies were founded: the Ministry of Information (MOI), principally for domestic consumption, and the Department of Propaganda to Enemy Countries, which later included enemy-occupied countries as well. The titular head of the latter organization was the politician Dr. Hugh Dalton. Its operational head was the ex-diplomat Sir Robert Bruce-Lockhart, who maintained that British propoaganda could be effective in Europe only if it were regarded as more accurate than that of the Nazis. Bruce-Lockhart also believed that, for the home front, exaggerated accounts of German weaknesses when the Wehrmacht was everywhere triumphant, had the reverse effect of that intended. Sir Robert had noted this mistake in connection with the Libyan campaign of 1941. Then, the first official army communiqués from Cairo had been almost lyrical in their optimism. The British propagandists, new to the job, had picked this up and made much of it in leaflets and broadcasts. But the offensive foundered and came to nothing, and the Germans made good capital out of the premature rejoicings.

Lockhart's department, whose official title was soon changed to Political Warfare Executive (PWE), was situated at Woburn in Bedfordshire. It was supposed to work in harmony with the BBC and the Ministry of Information in London, but its location 30 miles away from the capital did not facilitate liaison with these organizations. Hastily convened, its members were a motley crew—civil servants, barristers, university dons, journalists, army officers, advertising men, schoolmasters, and even a landscape gardener. The only thing these men had in common was that each was something of an expert on one or another of the European countries.

The first two years of PWE's existence could hardly be called encouraging. Bruce-Lockhart himself was always grumbling that they were achieving nothing. The cartoonist David Low, who did some work for PWE, was extremely caustic about it. One of his first wartime cartoons depicted the very efficient-looking Goebbels in a broadcasting studio, pouring out words into a microphone; next to him was Col. Blimp playing with a balloon. The caption ran:

"The worst cause in the world, and the best Propaganda;

The best cause in the world, and the worst Propaganda"

In his memoirs, Low relates that PWE officials showed him the type of leaflet they were dropping on Germany in the early days of the war, and asked him to do something like it. The leaflet he saw showed a Bavarian peasant in *Lederhosen* being told that Hitler had betrayed him to the Russians, and that as a result of Hitler, the Bolsheviks would soon come and take him away with all his crops. Low's acid comment was: "At that time with Hitler rampaging victorious, and the Russians practically hiding under the bed, I said it was one of the most foolish documents I had ever seen. And that if young men were risking their necks to drop this tripe over Germany, someone should be arrested."

On another occasion Low was commissioned by the Ministry of Information to design an image of Winston Churchill for the front of a Toby jug, which was to be sold in vast quantities in the United States. There was much official correspondence, congratulations, and admiration for this attempt to edulcerate Anglo-American friendship. A twin "Roosevelt jug" was even contemplated, but neither of the jugs ever got off the drawing board.

This inefficiency was also partly due to the multiplicity of commands. Lockhart's PWE team at Woburn was supposed to supervise the BBC broadcasts from London to foreign countries; but physical separation made control difficult, and the BBC was able to assert a virtual independence, broadcasting its own selection of material. Then there was the Ministry of Information, whose business was to look after home morale. In the first year of its existence it was under Duff Cooper, and was supposed to work in close collaboration with PWE. But Cooper could not abide Dr. Dalton; MOI and PWE were constantly at loggerheads. Duff Cooper says in his memoirs, "The main defect was

(*Top*) *The cartoons of David Low were the graphic expression of Britain's wartime conscience. In this 1937 cartoon he shows Anthony Eden courting Hitler and Mussolini, oblivious to the marching troops behind them.* (*Middle*) *Low envisioned Chamberlain ringing the death knell of democracy.* (*Bottom*) *The American cartoonist George Patzer was skeptical of Chamberlain's agreements with the Axis leaders.*

THE AUTOGRAPH COLLECTOR

WOULD YOU OBLIGE ME WITH A MATCH PLEASE ?

"GOOSE-STEPPING, NEVILLE ?"

(Below) The "Hitler jig" sequence, used in British and Commonwealth newsreels, was the repetition of a little triumphal hop Hitler made at Compiègne in 1940, when the French surrendered on the very spot where Germany had been humiliated at the end of World War I. The brief hop sequence was "looped" two or three times to make Hitler look as if he were dancing a comic jig.

that there were too few ordinary civil servants in MOI, and too many brilliant amateurs. The presence of so many able, undisciplined men in one Ministry was bound to lead to a great deal of internal friction."

Later, when Cooper was replaced by Brendan Bracken, things were hardly better. In the words of the unfortunate Bruce-Lockhart, who had to take their orders: "The weekly meetings frequently ended in a wrangle between Dr. Dalton and Mr. Bracken—which would have been quite amusing, had it not deferred all progress." In his book of memoirs, *Comes the Reckoning*, Bruce-Lockhart writes, "Indeed, during this period there was more political warfare on the home front than against the enemy."

It might appear from this that Lockhart had a thankless, even a hopeless, task—particularly as Churchill himself took only a spasmodic interest in propaganda. "This is a war of deeds, not words!" the great man was said to growl if the subject came up. Nor was Air Marshal Harris, the head of Bomber Command, which had to drop the leaflets on Germany, particularly keen on exposing his air crews to danger in order, as he put it, "to drop bits of bumph." Nevertheless as the war continued, and particularly after the first German reverses, PWE began to play a more effective role. Its propaganda methods improved so much that the American propaganda expert Harold Lasswell wrote, "Part of the superiority of British propaganda was due to its amazing suppleness. They were better psychologists than the Germans and Japanese. Where these Axis powers set such store by organization—sometimes damaging their cause by overorganization—the British applied improvisation and adaptation to good effect." This was of course largely due to the change of military fortunes. As Bruce-Lockhart said himself, "Propaganda is, or should be, easy for the winning side, and difficult for the losing side."

Lockhart's two principal instruments were the leaflet, dropped over enemy territory by Bomber Command, and the radio. The leaflets ranged from single sheets to miniature illustrated newspapers. A special feature of the leaflet operation was the miniature magazine. Reviews such as *La France Libre (Free France)* and a book of Churchill's speeches were reduced to the size of a folded handkerchief. Leaflets containing portions of the text of the Atlantic Charter also played an important part. Its signatories, Winston Churchill and Franklin Roosevelt, stated, "We seek no aggrandizement, territorial or otherwise. Our countries respect the principle of national self-determination, and look forward to a peace which will afford to every nation the means of dwelling in safety within its own boundaries." Millions of Europeans in German bondage heard or read these inspiring words.

Use of the radio was widespread, with broadcasts in 23 languages. Though broadcasting to the occupied countries was relatively easy, because their inhabitants were a ready audience for anything anti-German, devising broadcasts for Germany itself was more difficult. Here Churchill and Roosevelt did not help matters, by their unconditional surrender demand established at the Casablanca conference. This was a severe setback to PWE propaganda, which had aimed at separating the German people from their Nazi leaders. Indeed, the only propagandist who benefitted from the unconditional surrender declaration was Goebbels, who plastered the walls of the German cities with extracts from it, together with passages from Lord Vansittart's *Black Record*, a philippic against the German people as a whole. Goebbels told the Germans that even if some of them did not approve of the Nazis, the peace which the victorious Allies would now impose on them would make Versailles look like utopia.

In late 1942, when the Germans were suffering their first setbacks, PWE began to make use of a new psychological weapon —"black" propaganda, as distinguished from the conventional "white" propaganda. Briefly, "white" propaganda is addressed openly to the world, making much of the victories of one's own side and the defeats of the other. It aspires to uplift home morale with eyewitness accounts of military successes, regaling the audience with jokes and cartoons about the enemy and offering examples of the gallantry of one's own forces. It is based on truth, even if the truth is twisted a little. On the other hand, "black" propaganda is sheer invention or, as its detractors would say, "all lies." By disseminating false information in the enemy camp, military and civilian, it aimed at undermining morale and generally sowing doubt, disquiet, and depression.

A good example of white propaganda was the London broadcasts of the American radio commentator Edward R. Murrow during the 1940–41 blitz. The British had learned that America could not be cajoled into the war with the old 1916–17 propaganda methods. They realized that Murrow's broadcasts were exactly what they required in the circumstances and therefore gave him free rein and every facility, even access to Churchill should he desire it. Murrow's principle, he had announced himself, was "Just provide the honest news, and when there isn't any news, why—just say so. I believe people will like it like that."

Night after night as the bombs rained down on London, he broadcast "This is London" to his countrymen in America. He described the bombing simply and factually, always calm, never polemical, never urging an opinion. He knew, as did his English hosts, that he must show no bias; that the Americans still wanted to have no part in the war. But they had heard that England was weak and decadent, had seen how she was ignominiously expelled at Dunkirk—and yet, here was their own man describing how this people was standing up alone to the steady pummeling of the German Luftwaffe. Second only to Roosevelt, Murrow did as much as anyone to make the American people realize that they must not let England be defeated by the Nazis; otherwise, the implication was clear, they would soon have the bombs on their own heads. This was white propaganda at its best.

Another example of white propaganda in action was heard all over the world when Mussolini declared war on the United States in December 1941. He announced that "Italian soldiers will be proud to fight the Americans alongside the brave soldiers of the

(Top) The bulldog with Churchill's face was used more than once to signify British determination. (Bottom) Edward R. Murrow's radio broadcasts from London during the 1940–41 blitz told Americans of Britain's courage. On August 18, 1940, his broadcast concluded with the phrase, "the defense of Britain will be something of which men will speak with awe and admiration so long as the English language survives."

(Top) A German "black" parody of a British stamp on which the head of Stalin replaces that of King George. The word "Jewish" is intentionally misspelled. (Bottom) This German propaganda postcard picturing a British Tommy with four Arabs hanging from his bayonet was thought to have been dropped over Egypt. (Opposite page) British sardonic humor was aimed at the Nazis.

Rising Sun." Unfortunately, he forgot that he had used an identical phrase in 1917 when America came into the war on the side of the Allies. As editor of *Avanti*, he had written, "Italian soldiers will be proud to fight alongside the brave soldiers of the United States—the only nation in history which has never gone to war except in a just cause." The Italian experts of PWE used these contradictory statements to good effect, broadcasting both versions to Italy.

Hitler made a similar blunder which was pounced on by PWE when he confidently announced on October 10, 1941, that the war in Russia was over. The headlines of the Nazi Party newspaper *Völkischer Beobachter* read, "The Führer announces that the hour has struck! The war in the East has been won!" Thereafter on every anniversary of that date for the next three years, PWE dropped on Germany millions of facsimiles of the front page of the 1941 *Völkischer Beobachter*, with a red strip across it, "What Hitler said in 1941."

Black propaganda is quite different. It may seem a part of "British hypocrisy" that this people, who pride themselves on gentlemanly conduct, can, when under pressure, become so adept in double-dealing, misrepresentation, and every form of shady trickery that even Goebbels in his diaries had to admit a certain grudging admiration for them. Black propaganda is addressed entirely to the enemy, confusing him by exploiting if necessary his most sacred beliefs and feelings, such as a mother's concern for her son reported missing in active service. Its principal instrument, as used by Britain in World War II, was the so-called "secret" radio transmitter, actually in England, but purporting to come from dissatisfied elements of the Wehrmacht inside Germany.

The man who was put in charge of this black propaganda was Sefton Delmer, the *Daily Express* foreign correspondent. He knew Germany intimately and spoke the language like a native. From 1933 until the outbreak of the war he had been living there, and had covered the Nazis' activities for his paper. He knew Hitler and Goebbels personally and had been invited to accompany them on their political junketings. His department of the PWE employed various German speakers pretending to be spokesmen of the Wehrmacht, hard-boiled officers representing the opposition of the military caste to the party. They interspersed wild diatribes against the Allies, Britain and America, with tales of embezzlement and sexual deviation among the Nazi leaders. Some of these were probably the most pornographic ever put on the air. Sefton Delmer appealed, he said, to "the inner pig-dog in every German."

The black emissions were faithfully modeled on official German radio lines. They opened with patriotic music and the Wehrmacht daily communiqué. Then came a list of the latest Knight's Cross awards, followed by reports from the front in which the jargon of Goebbels' men was employed (e.g. "Terror raids by the RAF"). Then came the news, of which at least 90 percent was genuine, about the German advances in Russia, the destruction of Allied shipping, isolated air raids off the English coast,

LAST WILL AND TESTAMENT
OF
ADOLF HITLER

This is the Last Will and Testament of me
Mis-Leader of Germany—Better known as the
MAD DOG OF EUROPE.

———

Fearing that my end is near—that the Die is cast, that I have shot my bolt—
that I have now gone too far.

I GIVE AND BEQUEATH all my German People that believe in me to the *Dumb Peoples
League.*

I LEAVE my Swastika to Comrade Stalin, and he can do with it what he told ME to do
with it.

I BEQUEATH all my Medals to Goering, the weight of which, together with his own,
will bring him to his knees.

I LEAVE to Goebbels my stock of two Tons of Castor Oil, so he can carry on the tradition
of Purges.

I BEQUEATH "Mein Kampf" to Colney Hatch for further investigation.

I RETURN my Moustache to Charles Chaplin from whom I annexed it.

I BEQUEATH to Herr Ribbendrops my German Chamber which he may use by merely
raising his right hand in the customary manner.

I LEAVE to Goering the Roll of Linoleum which was given to me to put up my Corridor
together with numerous hot pokers and other sharp instruments.

AS I AM GOING to the place recommended to me by many of my dear public, I leave
my Torso to the Old Maids' Hostel.

ON MY DEATH I proclaim the annexation of HELL which I have tried to give to my
German people and rightfully belongs to the Fatherland.

I APPOINT Ribbendrops and Goering to be Executors of this, my Will, as they are well
experienced in Executions.

KNOWING my ultimate destination I wish to be buried in an Asbestos Suit.

Signed and Sealed with the upraised arm
in the form of the Naazti Salute.

adolf.

ADOLF THE PAINTER.

(Top) Posters were used to gain acceptance for a myriad of rules and regulations. (Bottom) Abram Games in his studio. Games fused contemporary artistic trends into powerful images. He believed that his war posters should make viewers think for themselves. His dramatic use of symbolism made his posters the most sophisticated of any produced during the war.

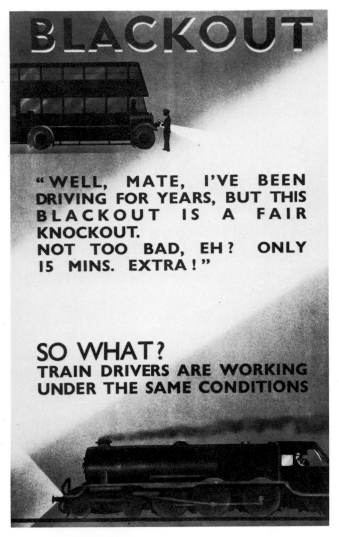

etc. But interspersed with this would be the invented item, stated simply without a word of comment.

For example, a typical black item concerned Goebbels' announcement that all bombed-out factory workers in a certain city would be given additional rations of food and, for their children, sweets. This was factual and reported as such; but the secret radio transmitter, calling itself *Soldatensender*, added that these extra rations contained special drugs to give the workers more energy. The aim of the black broadcasts was to keep the soldier at the front, the sailor at sea, the airman on the distant airfield in an occupied country, in a state of constant apprehension about the welfare of his family. Another device for the servicemen's benefit was to broadcast the names of the streets destroyed in a bombing raid the previous evening. The radio added that if the house of a sailor, airman, or soldier had been hit he could apply for compassionate leave. The soldier became extremely annoyed when he applied for leave, and it was refused because the authorities knew nothing about this dispensation.

To enhance the impression that *Soldatensender* was a German transmitter, Winston Churchill was occasionally referred to as "that flat-footed bastard of a drunken old Jew." Few Germans listening to this could conceive that British propagandists would dare to describe their country's leader in such terms.

Soldatensender sometimes announced that "the party bosses" were having a wonderful time feathering their own nests in soft billets far from the front while "our brave soldiers are freezing to death in Russia." Because of these officials' corruption, it said, the supply of winter clothing to the troops had been deliberately delayed.

Of these broadcasts Goebbels wrote in his diary, "The so-called *Soldatensender* which evidently originates in England and sometimes uses the same wavelength as our *Deutschlandsender* is certainly giving us something to think about. It does a clever job of propaganda, and from what is put on the air, one gathers that the English know exactly what they have destroyed in our cities."

Probably the most heartless of the deceptions, which Delmer himself says he felt ashamed of, was to obtain the name of a German soldier officially announced as dead, and write a letter to his mother from a "comrade" who had seen him alive and well in a neutral country, say Sweden or Switzerland, to which he had deserted. He naturally could not write himself. He was being extremely well treated and looked after, but she must on no account mention this to her friends. The delighted parents naturally gossiped, and many other soldiers imitated "the deserter" who was having such a good time. For the dead soldier's family, the reckoning came at the end of the war.

Among other black devices were letters to servicemen's families aimed at fostering distrust and dislike of high Nazi officials. Here the propaganda was based on true feelings, for everyone in Germany knew that these officials enjoyed—as high officials do everywhere—considerable perquisites denied to the man in the street. When a German soldier died in a hospital, the doctor sent a telegram by radio to the local party officer asking him to break the news to the dead man's family. This was intercepted by the PWE monitoring system, and a letter was written to the mother purporting to come from a "comrade" who had been with her son in his last hours. He described how right up to the end, her son expressed his faith in the Führer and Germany's ultimate victory. He then added that the dead man had mentioned a small possession, a ring, a watch, or a gold crucifix which he wanted his mother to have as a memento. He had sent it to the local party official, who would hand it over to her. Of course it never came, and it was clear to the family and their friends that the Nazi officials were "corpse robbers." As a variation on this theme, the writer sometimes added that the son had not died of his wounds as reported, but of a lethal injection administered by the medical officer who was a party member. The latter had decided that the patient could not recover, and his bed was wanted for another wounded soldier.

A black deception which had a direct military consequence explained why the Russians were fighting so well. It was all due to a new phosphorous shell with which the Americans had supplied them, and which could penetrate steel several feet thick; when it burst it burned up everything in sight. At the end of the war when the Cherbourg defenses were holding out desperately, it appeared that the American army would have the same problem defeating the Germans there as the Allies were having in the other French channel ports, where German units were obeying Hitler's order to fight to the last. The American commander at Cherbourg signaled to the leader of the German forces, General von Schieben, that it would be better for all concerned to surrender. To his surprise, the general replied that if they would fire one of "the new phosphorous shells" at the German fortress, he would be able to surrender honorably, as it was well known that there was no defense against them. Although no such shell of course existed, a pretense was made by firing a few incendiaries, whereupon the general surrendered with his garrison.

Occasionally the black methods had unwelcome repercussions. In mid-1942, when the Russians were under great pressure, a scheme was devised to relieve them by broadcasting to the French living on the Atlantic seaboard to evacuate and go inland, the object being to move German troops west against an invasion. Although this may have helped the Russians, when no invasion took place it had a bad effect on the morale of the French Resistance and on the French people in general. It also perplexed the Russians, who had supposed that some serious incursion was intended.

All these activities addressed to enemy countries came under PWE. Propaganda to the home front and Britain's allies abroad was the responsibility of the Ministry of Information, which had been instituted to inform the public about the war, and how they could help to win it. They had te be persuaded to volunteer for many onerous, boring, or dangerous jobs—to serve in war fac-

(Top) G. Lacoste did several humorous posters on the "careless talk" theme. Hitler was the butt of many British humorists. (Bottom) The London hoardings were thick with posters asking Londoners to lend a hand, save coal, and clean their plates. These exhortations worked for a while, but the public eventually found them excessive.

BEWARE

HE WANTS TO KNOW YOUR UNIT'S NAME.
WHERE YOU'RE GOING. WHENCE YOU CAME.
EVEN ALONE OR IN A CROWD
NEVER MENTION THESE OUT LOUD.

Posters for The Way Ahead *(Top) and*
San Demetrio London *(Bottom). These
films, which combined documentary
and fiction techniques, brought a new
honesty and integrity into British
wartime feature production. (Opposite
page) John Mills in Noël Coward's*
In Which We Serve, *an emotional film
about the crew of a destroyer which
was sunk in the Battle of Crete.*

tories, the Home Guard and the firefighting services, to "Dig for Victory," to economize in the use of transport and gasoline, to save waste paper, to observe food rationing and avoid the black market; above all, the ministry told Britons about the progress of the war without endangering national security. For these tasks it employed every publicity technique available—films, photographs, broadcasting, booklets, posters, press advertisements, exhibitions, public lectures. It recruited many distinguished publicists, artists, and writers. Among them was J. B. Priestley, the novelist and playwright, who delivered a series of stirring broadcasts on the BBC shortly after the fall of France.

For overseas, the ministry distributed British news, to ensure that material favorable to the British cause was given the widest publicity, and that enemy propaganda was immediately and convincingly denied. It also had a Press Censorship Department, to prevent the release of information likely to be of miltary value to the enemy. For the home press throughout the war this censorship was on a voluntary basis, in the sense that editors were not bound to submit their material, and the censors had no power to prohibit publication; but by obtaining the department's permission to publish, the newspaper concerned was protected from prosecution under the Defense Regulations should it inadvertently publish information of value to the enemy. For foreign and Commonwealth correspondents, submission to the censorship of outgoing cables was compulsory.

The Ministry of Information was also responsible for producing publicity material. For this it included a Campaigns Division, handling advertising and poster campaigns, and an Exhibitions Division designing and mounting anything from major exhibitions to small window displays, both at home and abroad. Such an exhibition in 1942 was "The Unconquerable Soul," displayed at the Charing Cross underground station. Its theme of resistance in occupied countries attracted record crowds. A Publications Division prepared and distributed a wide range of official illustrated books about the war, and promoted the circulation of British newspapers and periodicals abroad.

Word of mouth propaganda was recognized as most important, and the spreading of rumors carefully planned. The aim was to get people saying "I got it from a friend of mine," or "My boyfriend heard it in The Plumbers Arms . . ." This flattered the vanity of the hearer, who was encouraged to repeat what he believed to be a piece of red-hot news. In the words of Professor Lasswell describing how the British applied their pressure on a person-to-person basis to persuade America to enter the war: "The use of persons as channels of influence was most effective . . . information spread in the United States from businessman to businessman, journalist to journalist, professor to professor . . . It was all more subtle than in the 1914–1918 war . . ."

In Britain, as in all warring countries in World War II, the cinema played an important propaganda role. Great Britain entered the war with a well-trained group of documentary film makers. The film division of MOI made a series of weekly films

(Top) Desert Victory *was a documentary record of the North African campaign, which ended in Britain's first major triumph against Hitler.*
(Middle) In Which We Serve *appeared in 1942. The solidarity of a sunken ship's crew gave the British a feeling of unity when it was most needed.*
(Below) The Life and Death of Colonel Blimp *was based loosely on the cartoon characters created by David Low.*

lasting five minutes each, to be shown all over the country, interpolated into the normal program. The titles are self-explanatory—"Salvage with a Smile," "Hospital Nurse," "Speed the Plough." More important documentary films were made by the Crown Film Unit. A few, such as *Men of the Lightship*, aimed patently at stirring up feelings against the Germans. Lightships have always been regarded as exempt from attack in time of war, but the Nazis—according to this film—disregarded the chivalrous code. The lightship men, who have been machine-gunned, are shown swimming vainly for shore. Only one survives. Other documentaries featured British courage or military prowess. *Desert Victory*, about the battle of El Alamein; Humphrey Jennings' *London Can Take It*, about the blitz; and Harry Watt's *Target for Tonight*, about an RAF bombing raid on Germany. The latter film was produced in 1941 at a time when the British were tired of the "passive stoicism" theme and wanted to see more aggressive action. At least three compilation films were made from the footage of Leni Riefenstahl's Nuremberg rally film, *Triumph of the Will*. Charles Ridley's *Germany Calling* mocked the rally by showing SS and Wehrmacht troops parading to the rhythm of a popular English song, "Doing the Lambeth Walk."

Some films had a purely utilitarian purpose: how to get more eggs from your hens, how to breed rabbits for extra meat, how to enjoy a Woolton pie (Lord Woolton was the hapless Minister for Food), how to dig and hoe. This last film was supplemented by a MOI mobile exhibition which toured the country explaining how to grow more vegetables on one's patch, and how to store them. *Spring Offensive*, in spite of its martial title, was also about increasing the food supply by ploughing up pasture land—the whole seen through the naive eyes of a small boy evacuated from London.

Many feature films focused on the personal experience of war. The heroine of *They Also Serve* was a suburban housewife who quietly assumed all the burdens of daily life to free her men for the front and the factory. *San Demetrio London* was about the experience of a group of merchant seamen. Noel Coward's *In Which We Serve* was also about the fighting man—in this case the sailor. In a lighter vein was *The Life and Death of Colonel Blimp*, whose hero typified the stuffy British clubman's tendency to simply "muddle through."

Another pictorial field in which the British have always, since the days of Gilray and Rowlandson, been preeminent is the political cartoon; in the Australian-born David Low, Britain possessed one of the world's finest political cartoonists. His left-wing sympathies turned him violently against the Fascist dictators. In his autobiography he says that, although he was unaware of it at the time, his cartoon campaign against Hitler began as early as 1923. One of his general themes then was that if the Versailles powers continued to treat the new German Republic like Imperial Prussia, if they thwarted rather than fostered its growth, the German militarists would soon return to power. Here he was confirmed, he says, by the Ludendorf-Hitler putsch of 1923. It inspired a cartoon depicting Ludendorf standing arrogantly on the body of a prostrate Germany (Hitler was then comparatively unknown).

When Hitler and Mussolini achieved power, Low quickly realized that to satirize them as tyrants with blood dripping from their fingers, far from embarassing them, only gratified their vanity. What piqued them, he says, was to be depicted as clowns, or as what they were, upstart plebeians. This had been done by Cavalcanti in his film about Mussolini, *Yellow Caesar.* Mussolini appears not as an awesome despot, but as a ludicrous buffoon. Low, in his political cartoons, revealed the essential commonness of these "Johnny-come-latelys" to political grandeur.

When Lord Halifax visited Germany officially in 1937, he was told that the Führer was deeply offended by Low's cartoons of him, and that the paper in which they appeared, the *Evening Standard,* was banned in Germany. The subject of the cartoon responsible for this ban was Hitler's policy of undermining the authority of the League of Nations. Low showed Hitler attempting to set fire to it, above the caption, "It worked at the Reichstag. Why not here?" On Halifax's return to London, he summoned Low and told him that his cartoons were impairing the prime minister's policy of appeasement. Low obligingly desisted—but only for a few months. Soon afterward Hitler marched into Austria and Low, realizing that Chamberlain and Halifax had been fooled, took up his brush again with renewed vigor.

Other notable artists and draftsmen employed by MOI for propaganda included Cyril Kenneth Bird (Fougasse), the cartoonist whose humorous "Careless Talk" posters were among the best-known of the war. One showed two garrulous housewives sitting in a bus, with Hitler and Goering seated primly behind them, listening. Similar warnings were given by Abram Games, who designed posters for the War Office to be hung in barrack rooms, company offices, and other locations—"Careless Talk Kills," "Keep Your Big Mouth Shut," etc. The paintings of R. H. Talmedge commemorated the RAF's battles, while Bernard Partridge, the *Punch* cartoonist resurrected from World War I, returned to the pictorial attack on Germany in his traditional style.

In conclusion, what lessons did Britain learn about propaganda in World War II, to add to her experiences between 1914 and 1918? Broadly, that propaganda, apart from its black variety—which is not strictly propaganda but deception—should always be based on the truth, even though it may distort the truth. Secondly, that it should be under a unified control. In this respect Goebbels had the advantage throughout the war. Finally, it must never be obvious. The leaflets dropped on Germany at the beginning of the war made Hitler laugh. "What do the British take us for," he said, "as stupid as themselves?" In the words of the British propaganda expert Sydney Rogerson, "Propaganda that looks like propaganda is third-rate propaganda."

(Top) David Low drew Himmler and his followers as angels of death while the Nazi juggernaut rolled across Western Europe. (Bottom) Bernard Partridge had a more old-fashioned style. Hitler, pointing to the huge hollow dove, says to Goering, "This is my secret weapon, Herman, against the Allies. I got the idea from a nightmare."

THE ANGELS OF PEACE DESCEND ON BELGIUM

Sir Bernard Partridge, Punch, London

(Below) The tongue-in-cheek humor of Noël Coward's song, "Don't Let's Be Beastly to the Germans," lightened British spirits during the darker days of the war, when morale was low.

The bulldog symbol was revived to assert
British tenacity, c. 1942/U.S./Henri Guignon.

Heavy "Stirling" bombers raid the Nazi Baltic port of Lübeck and leave the docks ablaze

BACK THEM UP!

From a series of posters showing the British
forces in action, 1942/England/Roy Nockolds.

ARMS FOR RUSSIA . . . A great convoy of British
ships escorted by Soviet fighter planes sails into Murmansk
harbour with vital supplies for the Red Army.

An early expression of Anglo-Soviet solidarity,
c. 1942/England/Blake.

your **BRITAIN** · fight for it now

ISSUED BY A·B·C·A

This scene of the South Downs aroused feelings for an
idealized pastoral Britain, 1942/England/Frank Newbould.

*Humor appealed more to Britons than heavy-handed exhortations. One of the many
humorous treatments of the careless talk theme, no date/England/G. Lacoste.*

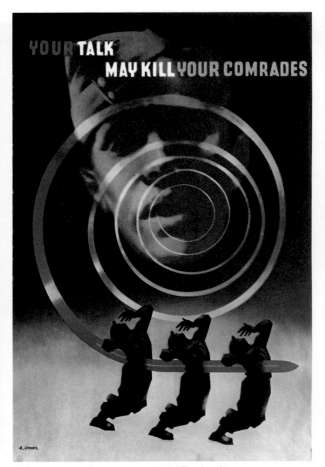

Soldiers were shown the results of loose talk,
c. 1942/England/Abram Games.

A famous wartime poster, 1942/England/
Abram Games.

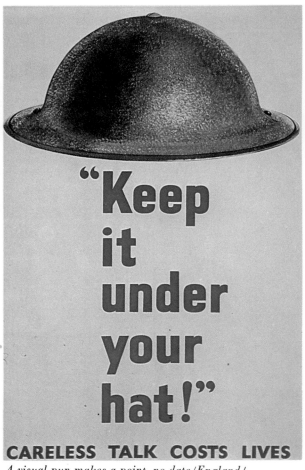

Another humorous treatment of the careless talk
theme, no date/England/G. Lacoste.

A visual pun makes a point, no date/England/
Artist unknown.

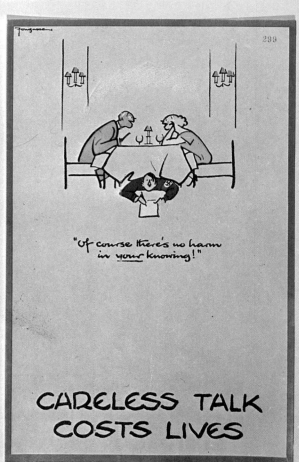

*Four variations on an important theme, no date/
England/Fougasse (Cyril Kenneth Bird).*

Many posters such as this urged care with
weapons, c. 1942/England/Abram Games.

Games' sophisticated designs expressed simple themes,
c. 1942/England/Abraham Games.

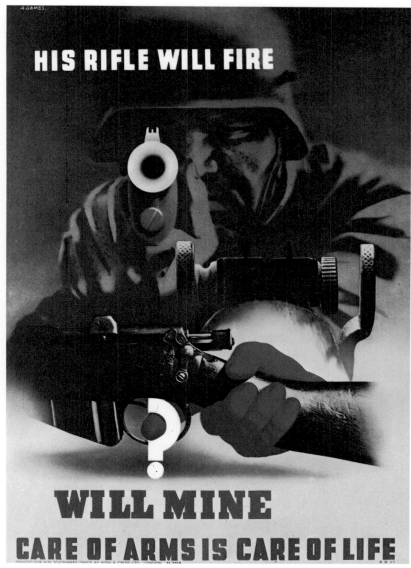

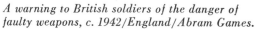

A warning to British soldiers of the danger of faulty weapons, c. 1942/England/Abram Games.

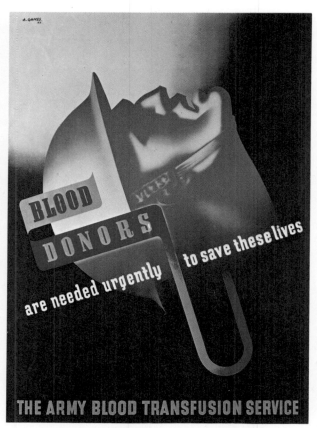

An urgent appeal for blood donors, c. 1942/ England/Abram Games.

He wanted to see inside

Accidents occur daily through wilful tampering. Taking ammunition to pieces is illegal, wasteful and dangerous.   Ask the expert.

Surrealism and photomontage are used to warn soldiers against accidents, c. 1942/England/Abram Games.

The skull and hat focused on the "easy" girl friend
as a VD source, c. 1943/England/Reginald Mount.

MAKE-DO AND MEND

says Mrs. Sew-and-Sew

ISSUED BY THE BOARD OF TRADE

Housewives were asked to make do with what they had, no date/England/Artist unknown.

BATTLE FOR FUEL

Turn it down
when you are warm

USE LESS GAS

A request for fuel economy from the Ministry of Fuel and Power, no date/England/Artist unknown.

A clear plate
means
A clear conscience

Don't take more than you can eat

Britons eventually had their fill of such homilies, no date/England/Fitton.

IS YOUR JOURNEY REALLY NECESSARY?

TICKETS

RAILWAY EXECUTIVE COMMITTEE

An appeal to avoid unnecessary travel, 1942/England/Bert Thomas.

I believe . . .

*A symbol of Christianity's power to conquer the
Nazis, no date/England/Artist unknown.*

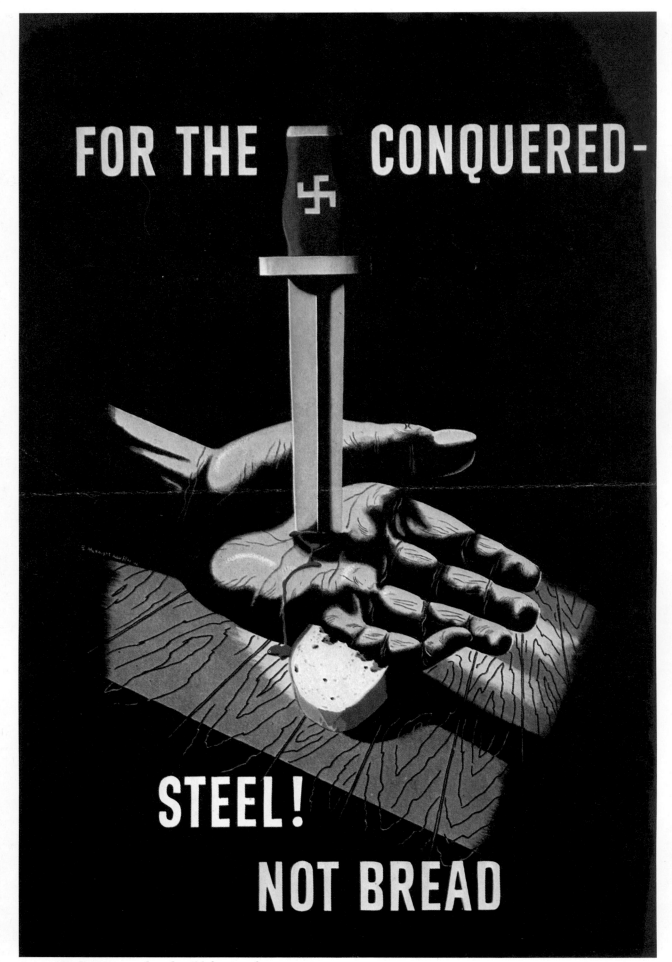

FOR THE   CONQUERED-

STEEL!
NOT BREAD

*A rare anti-Nazi image, though mild compared to
American efforts, no date/England/E. McKnight Kauffer.*

Stalin replaces Queen Elizabeth on this German anti-British
"black" parody, c. 1944/Germany/Artist unknown.

German "black" parody of a British stamp, c. 1944/
Germany/Artist unknown.

Poster for West Africa by a local artist, no date/
J. Olu Wright.

TRUFFLE EATER

by

OISTROS

2/6 NET

PRETTY STORIES

and

FUNNY PICTURES

Dust jacket for an illustrated "black" parody,
1940/England/Oistros

*Anti-Axis propaganda for the Middle East, no
date/England or Allies/Artist unknown.*

*An expression of British might after the tide had
turned, c. 1945/England/Sevek.*

THE UNITED STATES
ISOLATION AND INTERVENTION
1932-1945

CHAPTER FOUR

Although commercial advertising is developed and respected in the United States probably more than anywhere else in the world, its political counterpart, propaganda, has generally been neglected, even ignored. The American people, who have no objection to being prevailed upon to buy anything from toothpaste to a helicopter, balk at any attempt to influence them politically, particularly in foreign affairs. They regard propaganda as an alien, un-American, method of persuading people to subscribe to doctrines in which they have no interest. To most Americans in the 1920s and 1930s this suspicion was amply confirmed by the debased uses to which they saw propaganda being put in Europe, by the Fascists, Nazis, and Communists. Before mid-1940, no government-sponsored attempt to influence Americans about foreign affairs existed—for the very good reason that it would almost certainly have had the reverse of the effect intended.

There was also a perfectly good precedent. In World War I the American government had done nothing about propaganda until a week after the declaration of war in 1917. President Wilson then set up a Committee of Public Information under his friend, the well-known journalist George Creel, being careful however not to call it "propaganda." The committee played an important part in explaining to the American people why they were at war, and it even handled propaganda to the enemy, chiefly in the form of pamphlets distributed behind the lines. Nevertheless, as soon as the war was over, the committee was disbanded and its funds withdrawn. During its short and not inglorious existence it had been regarded with distaste by a section of Congress, by most American diplomats, and even by the secretary of state himself.

In the isolationist period between the wars, there was even less place for such a body. The Americans were disillusioned with the results of "the war to end wars," "the war to make the world safe for democracy." The treaty of Versailles seemed to have done little more than give birth to bellicose dictator states. Americans turned their backs on Europe. Many believed that there had been guilt on both sides, and that in 1917 they had been inveigled in by crafty British propaganda, by such slogans as "the fate of Western civilization is at stake," "the Hunnish barbarians," and stories about German troop atrocities in Belgium. When Great Britain and France went to war again with Germany in 1939, majority sentiment in America was to keep out, and propaganda from either side was considered suspect. In the words of the journalist Jay Allan, "In the Midwest you have the feeling that men are waiting with shotguns to shoot down the first propagandist who mentions Belgian babies." The greatest obstacle to Allied propaganda in World War II was the propaganda that preceded American entry into World War I.

This was the position when Franklin D. Roosevelt assumed the presidency in 1933. He was the first eminent American politician to be fully aware of the danger to America from the totalitarian states emerging in Europe. But he knew equally well that to persuade his countrymen of this would require time, tact,

While the Nazis overran Eastern and Western Europe, strong isolationist feelings kept America uninvolved until the Japanese bombed Pearl Harbor. (Top and middle) Impatience with the isolationists was expressed by cartoonists such as Clifford Berryman and Lute Pease. (Bottom) Kate Smith swelled American pride when she sang "God Bless America."

ALMOST THE LAST NEUTRAL.

PATIENCE WITH GERMANY

WONDER HOW LONG THE HONEYMOON WILL LAST?

and patience. In his broadcast to the American people in September 1939 he said what they wanted to hear—"This nation will remain neutral." But after describing the crisis which had led to war he added, "I cannot, all the same, ask every American to remain neutral in thought as well. Even a neutral cannot be asked to close his mind to conscience." He knew that, isolationist as most of them were, their sympathies lay with the democratic nations whose form of government they shared. An Institute of Public Opinion poll taken when World War II began revealed that 84 percent of the American public were in favor of an Allied, and only 2 percent in favor of an Axis, victory. But this was still a long way from wanting to fight on the Allied side.

The isolationists were a powerful force, consisting of many assorted elements—from the Protestant War Veterans of America, to the Catholic Irish-Americans; from midwesterners with a natural aversion to European commitments, to the large Italian community impressed by Mussolini's achievements; from Father Coughlin to Charles Lindbergh. The latter told a radio audience in September 1941, "The greatest advocates of bringing us into the war are the British, the Jews, and President Roosevelt." Other well-organized isolationist groups were the American Crusaders, the Silver Shirts, the Christian Front and, most powerful of all, the "America First" Committee which engaged one of the first New York advertising agencies, Batton, Barton, Durstine and Osborn, to mount a propaganda campaign against intervention and aid to Britain. Added to these were many socialists, opposed to British imperialism and her exploitation of India, and the Communist Party, just recovering from the sommersault they had been forced to turn following the Nazi-Soviet pact of August 1939. All these zealots emitted a stream of anti-British abuse and propaganda, which found a ready audience in a people who have always preferred peace to war.

The most voluble of the isolationists was Father Coughlin. Every week he broadcast to 3½ million Americans, warning them against the guile of the British and Jews. He said that President Roosevelt was a warmonger, and that his real name should be "Rosenfeld." He edited a well-written magazine, *Social Justice*, full of thinly veiled apologies for Nazi Germany. It had a circulation of half a million; and the St. Louis journalist, Marquis Childs, said that one of its articles was a word-for-word translation of a radio speech by Goebbels. Father Coughlin coined the phrase "the blood business" for those Americans who wanted to enter the war, he alleged, for financial gain. On February 19, 1940, his magazine published a manifesto entitled "Beware of the British Serpent," divided into sections each addressed to an ethnic group who had, allegedly, suffered at British hands; Polish-Americans, Irish-Americans, Italian-Americans. As a priest, Father Coughlin enjoyed a certain immunity from criticism, and he had a large following throughout the country.

As for the Nazis themselves, their propaganda problem in the United States was relatively simple (compared with that of the Allies). The Nazis knew they could expect no help of any kind

(Opposite page, top and bottom) Clifford Berryman and other cartoonists were skeptical of the 1939 Nazi nonaggression pact with the Soviets. (Top) Russia was portrayed as an aggressor nation before U.S. foreign policy did a volte-face when America entered the war and Russia became an ally. (Bottom) Father Coughlin and other pro-Nazi demagogues carried on an extensive propaganda campaign to keep America neutral.

(Top) A 1934 cartoon by Herblock,
who foresaw Hitler's ambitions of
conquest before most Americans took
the Nazis seriously. (Middle) Many
cartoonists treated Hitler as a joke.
(Bottom) Fritz Kuhn, leader of
the German-American Bund. The Bund
attracted many German sympathizers
in the late 1930s, but collapsed in
1939. (Opposite page, top and bottom)
Registration forms for Bund members
and sympathizers.

DER FUEHRER

DICTATORSHIP

from America. They could, however, by encouraging groups
like Father Coughlin's, neutralize America, so that she would
give help inadequately, or not at all, to Britain and France. But
they started from a number of dubious premises. They believed
that of all the democracies America was potentially the most
anti-Jewish; they thought they could count on the support of a
number of native anti-Semitic groups, such as the Klu Klux
Klan, the Crusaders for America, the Paul Reveres, the American Patriots, Inc. They also believed that the large colony of
German descent, some 20 million, would be firmly on their side.
For this purpose Goebbels had created and encouraged the German-American Bund, which was headed by Fritz Kuhn, a fanatic
German who had migrated to the United States in the late 1920s.
But the Nazis were never renowned for their subtlety (indeed
they openly scorned it), and here they overplayed their hand.
The Jewish pogroms in Germany and the Nazis' vicious anti-
Semitic propaganda only alienated Americans, whatever their
personal feelings about Jews. Also, the Nazis do not seem to
have fully understood that the United States is not Sweden. They
had mesmerized the smaller nations of Europe into terrified in-
action with their threatening propaganda—such fearful films as
Baptism of Fire about the Polish campaign—and their belief
that the "big lie" if repeated often enough will finally be believed. But the Americans proved singularly unimpressed by the
big talk, which only served to strengthen anti-Nazi feeling. It
soon became impossible for a Nazi propagandist to appear on an
American platform; and even first generation German-Amer-
icans were quick to dissociate themselves from the German-
American Bund (whose demise came in 1939 when Fritz Kuhn
was indicted and imprisoned for stealing the organization's
funds). The "blood calls to blood" propaganda which had been
so successful in certain European countries made little impression in the United States.

In spite of this, the problems which confronted President
Roosevelt after the fall of France in 1940 were prodigious. For
Americans to be negative about Germany did not necessarily
mean that they were positive about Germany's enemies. To convince his countrymen that Britain must at all costs be saved for
America's own safety proved to be extremely difficult. More-
over, it is far harder to persuade people in a democracy than in
a dictatorship. The latter possesses the great advantage that
decisions can be taken swiftly and acted on at once. These in turn
require that the people are ready to accept them without hesita-
tion; this they do thanks to having been properly indoctrinated
before. But in the democracies there is, far from unhesitating
acceptance of the leaders' decisions, frequently criticism of
them. Although in wartime internal conflicts are most damaging,
in the democracies they cannot be suppressed. All democratic
propagandists can hope for is to persuade people that for the
duration of the war it is best not to exercise their inalienable
rights—the right to grumble, to reject conscription, to be pac-
ifists or conscientious objectors, the right to hate blacks, Cath-
olics, Jews, the right to grow flowers instead of potatoes in the

German American Bund

ADDRESS: GERMAN AMERICAN BUND, P. O BOX 1, STATION "K", NEW YORK, N. Y.

DISTRICT: ....
SECTION: ....
UNIT: ....
ADDRESS: ....
....

Application for Membership

*) Payable when applying

Initiation Fee $1.00
Monthly Dues $0.75
Voluntary Donation $0.50 up

I hereby apply for admission to membership in the „German American Bund". The purposes and aims of the Bund are known to me, and I obligate myself to support them to the best of my ability. I recognise the leadership principle, in accordance to which the Bund is being directed. I am of Aryan descent, free from Jewish or colored blood.
Please write distinctly.

Full Name .... Occupation: ....

Exact Address .... Telephone: ....

Born .... Place of Birth: .... Single/Married, Widowed: ....
    Day   Month   Year

First Papers No .... What Court and when obtained: ....

....

Final Papers No.: .... What Court and when obtained: ....

....

When and where immigrated: .... Passport No.: ....

Two References: (1) ....

(2) ....

To what Organizations do you belong? ....

Only U. S. Citizens are eligible for office. First Papers suffice for Membership in "Prospective Citizens' League"

Paid Dues
Initiation Fee .... $:............
Monthly Dues .... $:............
Vol. Donation .... $:............

Date: ....

....
Applicant's Personal Signature

....
Unit Leader

Please do not use this space
No. ....

German American Bund

ADDRESS: GERMAN AMERICAN BUND, P. O BOX 1, STATION "K", NEW YORK, N. Y.

DISTRICT: ....
SECTION: ....
UNIT: ....
ADDRESS: ....
....

Sympathizer's Registration

*) Payable when registering

Registration Fee $1 00
Monthly Contribution $0 75
Voluntary Donation $0 50 up

I hereby register as a Sympathizer of the "German American Bund". The Aims and Purposes of the Bund are known to me and I obligate myself to support them to the best of my ability. I am of Aryan descent, free from Jewish or Colored Blood.

Name: ....

Address: ....

(The address need not be given. A Pseudonym may be used.)

Date: ....

Paid
Initiation Fee .... $:............
Monthly Contribution . $:............
Vol. Donation .... $:............

....
Applicant's Personal Signature

....
Unit Leader

Please do not use this space
No. ....

(Top, bottom, and opposite page)
Three cartoons by Daniel Fitzpatrick
of the St. Louis Post-Dispatch.
Fitzpatrick's powerful images of the
German juggernaut brought home the
dangers of Nazi expansion.

ORIENTAL END OF THE AXIS.

THURSDAY, JULY 10, 1941.

TO WHOM IT MAY CONCERN:

SATURDAY, SEPTEMBER 28, 1940.

back garden.

Propaganda is also more difficult to organize in democratic countries, because lies can be more easily exposed than in dictatorships. The big lie cannot be continually repeated or it will become ludicrous and have the reverse effect. Therefore the attitude adopted by the propaganda department which President Roosevelt set up in 1940 (naturally not under that name) was that it must always retain the essence of truth in what it said. It could embroider the truth, but there must be some truth to embroider.

In November 1940, he had sent Colonel Donovan on a recconaissance tour of the principal warfronts. On a visit to Britain he was introduced to the newly formed British Psychological Warfare Department. He reported so favorably on this to the president that in July 1941 Roosevelt appointed him Coordinator of Defense Information; he immediately set up a political warfare department. By the time of Pearl Harbor, this was already in action, and thereafter it functioned with growing effectiveness. The organization was at first known as the Office of Facts and Figures, and its chief function was to explain the need for helping the Western democracies with as much aid as possible short of war. Its main theme was that a Germany victorious in Europe would be strong enough to flout the Monroe doctrine and—with the British fleet eliminated—would launch an attack on South America. Here, the propagandists knew, American public opinion was particularly sensitive. Robert Sherwood, the playwright and a staunch interventionist, was enrolled as a propagandist; he announced, "If Great Britain is defeated, then the next war will follow quickly, and it will be fought in this hemisphere." Another eloquent Anglophile was the journalist Dorothy Thompson; she was an interventionist not, she said, for Britain's sake, but for America's.

In Germany, Goebbels controlled the entire propaganda apparatus in every media, which responded instantly to the touch of his hand on the tiller. In the United States, as in Britain, propaganda was bedevilled by a multiplicity of squabbling departments, often fighting one another more than the enemy. The Americans repeated and aggravated British mistakes by setting up two psychological warfare departments, the Office of War Information (OWI) and the Office of Strategic Services (OSS), the first with responsibility for overt or "white" propaganda, the second for covert or "black" propaganda. Both groups wanted to gain the ear of the president, who did not improve matters by granting them charters which were vague in defining their respective spheres of authority.

At the head of OWI was Elmer Davis, a well-known radio commentator. His task was not made easier by Washington because a sizable element in Congress still regarded propaganda as a kind of wasteful mumbo jumbo. He was even accused of using his organization to advance the cause of the Democratic party—presumably because Roosevelt had set it up. In fact, Davis was always complaining that he could hardly ever have access to the president to obtain rulings. His staff, which had

WINGS OVER EUROPE.

WEDNESDAY, MAY 15, 1940.

The "Safe Conduct Pass" was one of the most successful leaflets devised by the Office of War Information. The leaflets were snapped up by German and Italian soldiers in North Africa because they were assured of being well looked after and removed from the danger zone.

been hastily cobbled together in 1942, contained, inevitably, a large foreign element, some of whom were prima donnas more concerned with propagating themselves than America. This gave fuel to the well-known American suspicion of "foreign intellectuals." He also had friction with the services' high command, whose generals and admirals regarded propaganda much as they did psychiatry, unnecessary and unmanly. In November 1942, at the time of the invasion of North Africa, General Eisenhower said, "I don't know much about psychological warfare, but I want to give it a chance." After the war, the Army General Board, in its final report, concluded that "propaganda has been a neglected and ineptly used political and diplomatic weapon."

The American propaganda bodies clearly could not compare, at least at the outset, with Goebbels' mammoth and monolithic structure. But the Americans, slow to anger, when finally roused are unstoppable, particularly in spheres which they regard as their own. In two of these during World War II, they surpassed all other nations in propaganda achievment. One was the use of the leaflet for offensive propaganda, and the other, films for domestic consumption.

In wartime when frontiers are closed, the leaflet dropped from the air is the surest way of getting at enemy civilian morale. (Radio of course is another, but many people are frightened of listening to forbidden foreign radio stations.) But when things are going badly in the war, and wherever you turn in the street or the countryside you find leaflets telling you day after day, week after week, in the simplest terms what is happening in the war, it soon has a cumulative effect. The Americans used the leaflet to announce facts without commentary, telling the Europeans in the tersest terms what their leaders were concealing from them—the territory gained by the Allies, the progress of the war in the various theaters. Here the vast American airfleets that dominated the skies literally swamped the enemy cities with paper.

A special squadron of Flying Fortresses was set aside to do nothing but carry out leaflet raids. During the last years of the war, the OWI was showering occupied Europe with 7 million leaflets a week (compared to the total of 3 million American leaflets distributed throughout all of World War I). A young American air force captain, James Monroe, made this possible by inventing a leaflet bomb—a cylinder of laminated paper, five feet long and one and a half feet in diameter, which could hold 80,000 leaflets. When the bomb had fallen to a height of 1,000 feet, an automatic fuse opened it, the leaflets were released and fell concentrated on the target. Before his invention, the leaflets were simply tossed out of the bomb hold from a great height and dispersed far and wide.

On July 10, 1943, 7 million of these leaflets were scattered on German and Italian positions in preparation for the Sicilian invasion. A few days later on July 16, millions more were dropped in every part of Italy, informing the Italians that they could either die for Mussolini and Hitler, or live for Italy. On August 15, 1944, they were dropped in similar numbers on

German troops in southern France. Some leaflets were in the form of "safe conduct" passes for enemy soldiers, luring them to desert with promises of good treatment and illustrations of this treatment in comfortable surroundings away from the front. The "safe conduct" passes always contained a box written in English instructing the American soldiers whom they approached with the leaflets: "The man who carries this leaflet is no longer an enemy. Under International Law, you will ensure that he is guaranteed personal safety, clothing, food, living quarters and if necessary medical attention." Other leaflets contained instructions on how to malinger or feign illness. Others came in the form of counterfeit ration cards, coupons, stamps, and currency. All these operations on so vast a scale were made possible, it should be noted, by one main factor, the vast airplane production of the American factories.

Aerial supremacy was used again for dropping on France a tabloid newspaper produced by OWI called *L'Amérique en Guerre* (*America at War*). It described factually the American war production figures, the weapons and ships being turned out daily, hourly, by the greatest industrial power in the world. It listed Allied advances with names of places in North Africa, Sicily, and Italy now in Allied hands. By D-Day 1944, 7 million copies of this journal were being dropped weekly in France. Similar newspapers were delivered to Norway, Spain, and Ireland.

In mid-1944 the leaflet hailstorm was diverted to Germany itself. One side of one leaflet bore the American flag, the other the ominous words, "Adolf Hitler declared war on the United States on December 11, 1941." Later, a news tabloid *Sternebanner* (*The Star-Spangled Banner*) was dropped weekly on the German cities. On the lines of *L'Amérique en Guerre* it too was strictly factual—so factual that it occasionally carried news unfavorable to the Allies. This raised objections in high Allied military circles; but it made *Sternebanner* credible to its German readers because, as OWI had reasoned, credibility could not be achieved without objectivity. Another German-language paper, *Frontpost*, was also distributed weekly on the Italian front by shellfire as well as by air. That so much artillery and air power could be diverted from their usual deadly business was in itself, to the enemy soldier, a depressing sign of the vast armaments mounted against him.

Ronald Seth, in his book *The Truth Benders*, says that each leaflet was read by at least six people, and that there could have been very few men, women, and children in the occupied countries who did not see them. One important reason why they were read eagerly was because they were often essential to the safety of the civilian. They often gave a warning of coming bombing attacks, thus allowing time to leave the area and harm's way. They were used in this way at Monte Cassino, when all civilians who were sheltered in the monastery were warned twenty-four hours before the attack began.

The second propaganda medium which was particularly effective in wartime America was the radio. It has always been

The Japanese attack on Pearl Harbor, December 7, 1941, was the decisive blow that brought the United States into World War II. (Top) A recording of President Roosevelt's address to the Congress on December 8, 1941. (Middle) Roosevelt kept the public informed of the war's progress through his quiet, intimate "Fireside Chats." (Bottom) Sammy Kaye's rendition of "Remember Pearl Harbor" fostered patriotic feelings.

(Below and opposite page)
After the United States entered World
War II, songwriters began to turn
out music to keep spirits up on the
home front. Styles ranged from popular
ditties to semireligious spirituals.
People danced to "Goodbye Mama—
I'm Off to Yokahama" and other tunes
played by the swing orchestras of the
day.

more important in America than in smaller countries because her vast size precludes any newspaper's having a national circulation. Radio alone could create a truly national public opinion. Also, the special radio announcers and commentators in America were given much freer license than their European counterparts. They have developed to a high pitch the art of playing on the emotions of the public.

It is appropriate that the American who did more than anyone else to bring his country into the war on the side of the Allies should also have been its finest radio speaker—President Roosevelt. His mastery of the medium dates back to the early 1930s, when he persuaded a recalcitrant public that the New Deal was their only salvation. On March 12, 1933, he inaugurated his famous series of radio "fireside chats" from his room in the White House. Unlike Hitler and Mussolini, who also took every advantage of the new medium to expound their views, and whose bombastic radio speeches were made against a background of mass hysteria, Roosevelt preferred a more intimate approach. He spoke calmly, sharing his thoughts and ideas with, as it were, all the families of America. Many felt he was talking to them personally, and that he understood their problems. By his measured tones they felt assured that he was at once their leader and their friend. During the Depression these chats helped the New Deal, "this socialist measure" as a hostile Congress often called it, to become law.

Evidence of the success of the fireside chats came by mail after each broadcast. Before them, the presidential mail had been handled by one secretary. After March 1933, half a million unanswered letters piled up in the White House, and the secretarial staff had to be greatly enlarged. Radio was the medium, too, with which after September 1939 President Roosevelt again addressed a recalcitrant audience, telling them that if Britain were defeated they would soon have to face the greatest danger in their history—the European continent united at last under the most bellicose power in the world.

Apart from Roosevelt's fireside chats, American radio in the period September 1939–December 1941 had remained as far as possible neutral, avoiding great controversial European issues. After Pearl Harbor this quickly changed. So frightened were many people living on the West Coast that they demanded the immediate incarceration or removal to the interior of the considerable Japanese-American colony living peaceably there. The fear of a Japanese invasion may not have been entirely justified, but it at least woke up the West and Midwest, the traditionally isolationist areas of the country.

In February 1942 "This is War," a 13-week series produced by Norman Corwin, began. It aimed at inspiring, informing, and ultimately frightening people into action. The titles of the series were self-explanatory—"The Enemy," "America at War," "Your Navy," "Your Army," "The United Nations," "Mr. Smith against the Axis." The series was broadcast on all the nationwide networks every Saturday night, and was heard by some 20 million Americans. It was also short-waved to the

VICTOR

P 20-1   26516-A

BALLAD FOR AMERICANS—Part 1
(John Latouche–Earl Robinson)
Paul Robeson, Basso
American People's Chorus
directed by Earl Robinson
Victor Symphony Orchestra
conducted by Nathaniel Shilkret

COLUMBIA

36445
(CO 31647)

(There'll Be Bluebirds Over)
THE WHITE CLIFFS OF DOVER
Fox Trot - Vocal Chorus by
Harry Babbitt and Glee Club
-Burton-Kent-
KAY KYSER and
his ORCHESTRA

COLUMBIA

For perfect tone
use Columbia Needles

36640
(HCO 904)

PRAISE THE LORD AND PASS THE
AMMUNITION!
Fox Trot-Vocal Chorus by Glee Club
-Loesser-
KAY KYSER and
his ORCHESTRA

BLUEBIRD

For best results
use Victor Needles

B-10881-A

THERE'LL ALWAYS BE AN ENGLAND
(Parker-Charles)
The Happy Gang
Vocal by Eert Pearl with chorus by Bob Farnon,
Eddie Allen, Blain Mathe and
Kathleen Stokes at the organ

VICTOR

For best results
use Victor Needles

27407-B

BLESS 'EM ALL—Vocadance
(Hughes-Lake-Stillman)
Barry Wood and The Four King Sisters
with Orchestra

VICTOR

For best results
use Victor Needles

20-1661-A

BELL BOTTOM TROUSERS–Fox Trot
(Moe Jaffe)
Tony Pastor and his Orchestra
Vocal refrain by Ruth McCullough
and Tony Pastor

*Every popular art form was a
propaganda medium during the war.
(Top) Al Capp promoted the national
campaign to save fat and scrap metal.
(Bottom) A recruiting poster in
comic-strip style.*

rest of the world. By 1943, of the twenty N.B.C. serials which went out weekly, only five were unconnected with the war. Some, such as the one featuring Ma Perkins who lost a son in the fighting, were aimed at the home front; she was constantly telling housewives to save fat and collect tinfoil. The results were encouraging. By August 1942, fat and grease salvage had increased by 3 million pounds, and by March 1943 by 7½ million pounds. Victory gardens for home-grown food-stuffs were dug by an extra 2 million families. Information about war bonds, victory loan, Red Cross, victory food, student nurses, and shoe rationing was heard by millions of listeners. After a two-week appeal, 30,000 Grade-A glider pilots volunteered for the air force. The OWI, which organized this radio campaign, claimed that each adult in the United States heard four war messages a week. The radio was also used offensively in the theaters of war. The Italian navy in 1943, after being urged by American radio broadcasts every quarter of an hour to deliver itself to the Allies, did so. Of this, a British admiral commented that the American radio propagandists had "accomplished in one day" what he had not been able to do for three years.

Though the poster could make no claim to competition with radio in its influence on the American public, nevertheless a barrage of posters was issued by assorted government agencies and private corporations during the war years. They exhorted factory workers to boost their production, warned civilians against careless talk, and encouraged everyone to help defeat the enemy. Posters were commissioned from such prominent artists and designers as Ben Shahn, Normal Rockwell, and David Stone Martin, but well-designed as these were, they could hardly influence the public as much as the day-to-day events to which it was exposed through radio, newsreels, and newspapers.

Among newspaper cartoonists, Daniel Fitzpatrick of the *St. Louis Post-Dispatch,* Herblock, and others had continued throughout the 1930s to remind Americans of events in Europe. Fitzpatrick gave the swastika a menacing interpretation by drawing it as a huge steamroller and as a greedy octopus stretching its tentacles across the English Channel. Cartoons by Lute Pease and Clifford Berryman showed the continuing pressure on Uncle Sam to absolve his neutrality. After Pearl Harbor, the key events in Europe and the Pacific were interpreted for the public by many cartoonists in newspapers throughout the country. Bill Mauldin's grubby, mud-soaked G.I.s, Willy and Joe, served as a reminder that war was anything but heroic. Mauldin's cartoons implicitly asked the people to support the men in uniform, who were enduring untold hardships to preserve the democratic way of life.

Another domain in which American propaganda distinguished itself during the war was film. Goebbels had realized its immense importance years before, making it his special province. But when the war began he could not compete with Hollywood. Film is the American art—or craft—par excellence. Each week 85 million Americans sat in the blackened halls for hours. In the magniloquent but only too justified boast of a Hollywood tycoon, "Influence is exerted by Hollywood over the thought processes and emotions of 120 million Americans. The clothes that are worn by Hollywood today are worn by the nation tomorrow. The games that are played in the parlors of the Hollywood great become the pastimes of America. That which is done by Hollywood today will be emulated by American cities big and small, and by the citizens who live in them." It was clear that this formidable weapon must be enlisted in the service of its country—but how? The Hollywood moguls were particularly independent-minded men.

For decades Hollywood had been turning out between six and seven hundred films a year, principally domestic comedies, westerns, police thrillers, romances, and musicals. They were addressed to the more primitive emotions—which was of great value in making the change from peace to war production easier than had been expected. Hollywood, with its strong Jewish and British elements, was overwhelmingly on the side of the Allies, and it wanted to do what it could to help them—but of course in such a capitalist organization, without sacrificing profits. For this reason, any war propaganda contained in a Hollywood film had to be incidental to the entertainment. Americans went to the cinema to be thrilled, harrowed, amused; they were unreceptive to political propaganda. It was soon found that the stereotyped mystery thriller lent itself admirably to Nazi fifth-column stratagems, as did mobland shootings to Nazi cruelty. The "bad guy" gangster became the "bad guy" Nazi; while the hero, the clean-cut, upstanding American could become the clean-cut, upstanding British fighter pilot (or a young American who had volunteered for the RAF). Single-handed they outwitted scores of Nazis and purloined the secret plans for the Nazis' new deadly ray gun or secret new explosive. The Nazis, on the other hand, were not capable of much more than taking pot shots at defenseless pilots as they floated down to earth on their parachutes.

Simple-minded plots were nowhere more prevalent than in the serials, which theaters showed in installments over a period of weeks to accompany the features. In *Secret Service in Darkest Africa*, the hero, Rex Bennett, has a life-and-death duel with a Nazi. After disposing of him he throws his sword into a portrait of Adolf Hitler. Other stock characters in the serials were Spiderman, Batman, Spy Smasher, the Masked Marvel, Secret Agent X-9, and the Jungle Queen, who stymied Nazi plans for taking over Africa. Once the United States became involved in the fighting, even Tom Mix was enlisted to have a go at the Japanese. One of his films depicted a giant King Kong who terrorized the countryside; he turned out to be a huge balloon manipulated by Japanese agents.

More serious films, such as Chaplin's satirical *The Great Dictator* (1940), *Mrs. Miniver*, showing the stoicism of Britain under the blitz, and *The Moon is Down*, about the ruthless Nazi occupation of Norway, became immensely popular—although they were very powerful, if veiled, political propaganda. In 1940 the America First Committee had attacked Hollywood for incorporating anti-Fascist propaganda in films such as *Confes-*

(Top) A biting caricature of the Axis leaders by Arthur Szyk. (Middle) An unsuccessful poster by Jean Carlu to increase factory production. Workers thought the top figure was a gangster because of his cap. (Bottom) Bill Mauldin's Willy and Joe were reminders to the folks at home that war was a tough grubby business.

"Just gimme a coupla aspirin. I already got a Purple Heart."

German emigré actors found work in Hollywood as Nazi officers. (Top, left) Conrad Veidt as General Kurt von Kalb in Escape. *(Top, right) Peter Lorre in* Cross of Lorraine. *(Bottom) Erich von Stroheim in* North Star. *(Opposite page) Helmut Dantine in* Edge of Darkness, *a melodrama about the Norwegian resistance.*

sions of a Nazi Spy (1939), which exposed the danger of a fifth column in the United States. The movie men countered that they had always catered to popular taste commercially and this is what they were still doing.

By 1943 three out of ten films made in Hollywood were connected with the war. After the Nazi invasion of the Soviet Union, the United States did an about-face and Hollywood began producing films which glorified the Soviets, or at least treated them sympathetically. *North Star* (1943) was probably the first serious attempt to portray Soviet Russia on the American screen.

Hitler, Mussolini, Tojo, and their followers were also the butts of much film humor. They even appeared in cartoons, where they were outwitted by the likes of Bugs Bunny and ridiculed by Donald Duck in Walt Disney's *Der Führer's Face.*

Until the war, the documentary or information film had hardly been able to compete commercially with the Hollywood entertainment film. Among the small number of the former was the series *March of Time,* which began in 1935 and appeared monthly. Produced by the publishers of *Time* magazine, it was in theory impartial, but the antitotalitarian atmosphere was clear in the accompanying commentary. For this reason it ran into much criticism in isolationist circles.

When the Japanese bombed the U.S. Navy gunboat *Panay* on the Yangtze River in 1937, Universal and Fox Movietone cameramen were on the spot. Their film was rushed back to the United States and attracted large crowds when it was shown in theaters across the country, accompanied by a soundtrack opposing Japanese militarism. About the same time, a film about the bombing of Shanghai made by Fox Movietone was openly partisan. At one point it showed a helpless crying baby whose parents had been killed in the attack. That baby's pathetic face was seen by 136 million Americans. But these films were exceptions. Before the war, foreign politics were seldom seen on American screens. In fact, the intense desire to avoid controversy led Pennsylvania film distributors to enter into an agreement in 1936 that no newsreel bearing on political issues would be seen in their theaters.

But as the war in Europe continued, the people turned gradually away from the isolationist view, and more and more documentaries and newsreels were shown. By the time the United States entered the war the motion picture industry, as well as the public, was taking documentaries seriously for the first time. Within a matter of months of the American entry, Hollywood directors including Frank Capra—who was summoned to Washington to see the president—were producing documentary films explaining the war and why the totalitarian states had to be defeated. Capra gathered a talented team of directors around him: Anatole Litvak, John Huston, and Eric Knight. His famous series "Why We Fight" was made to explain to the American fighting man the background of the war up to America's entry. *Prelude to War* (1942) described the rise of Fascism, Nazism, and Japanese militarism between 1931 and 1938. *The Nazis Strike* (1943) dealt with events in Central Europe from the Aus-

Hollywood producers manufactured their own version of World War II. (Left, top to bottom) Robert Young (left) and Dan Dailey, Jr. in The Mortal Storm; *Otto Kruger (seated) and Tim Holt in* Hitler's Children. *(Right, top to bottom) Erich von Stroheim (left) in* Five Graves to Cairo; *Skippy Homeier (right) in* Tomorrow, the World; *George Sanders in* Confessions of a Nazi Spy; *Raymond Massey (seated) and Henry Daniell in* Hotel Berlin; *Otto Preminger in* The Pied Piper. *(Opposite page, top row, left to right) Humphrey Bogart in* Sahara; *John Garfield (left) and Alan Hale in* Destination Tokyo; *Richard Conte in* Guadalcanal Diary. *(Middle row, left to right) Burgess Meredith in* The Story of G.I. Joe; *Irene Dunne and Alan Marshall in* The White Cliffs of Dover; *Tallulah Bankhead in* Lifeboat. *(Bottom row, left to right) Rains, Henreid, Bogart, and Bergman in* Casablanca; *The Andrews Sisters in* Buck Privates.

A full array of heroes and villains appeared in American war films. (Left, top to bottom) Dana Andrews in The Purple Heart; *Cary Grant in* Destination Tokyo; This is the Army. *(Right, top to bottom)* Song of Russia; *Walter Huston in* Mission to Moscow; *Robert Watson as Hitler in* The Hitler Gang. *(Bottom and opposite page) Charlie Chaplin as Adenoid Heynkel in* The Great Dictator.

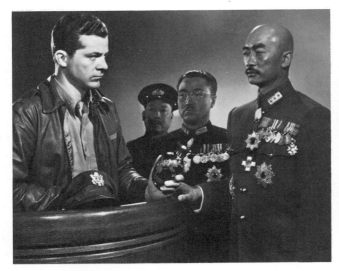

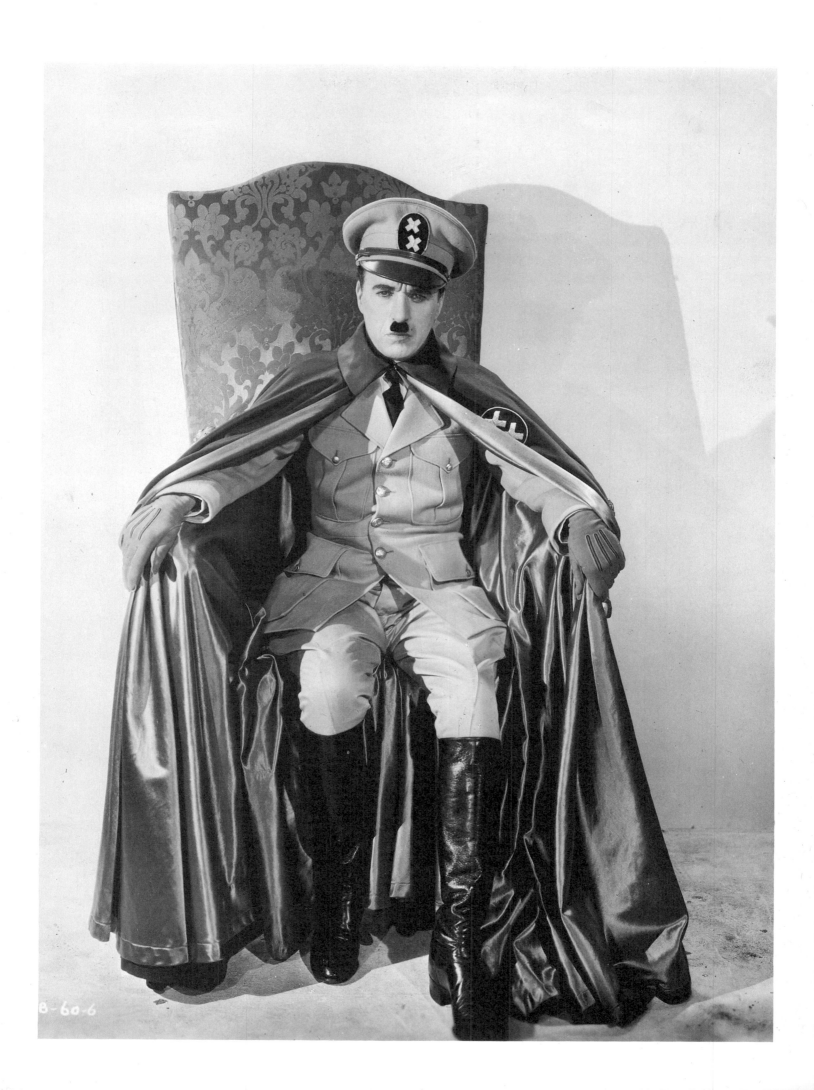

(Top) The song "Der Führer's Face" was a high-spirited poke at Hitler. (Middle and bottom) Victory through Air Power, Walt Disney's cartoon for the Air Force. (Opposite page, top and bottom) Donald Duck in Disney's Der Führer's Face. (Following page, top) Frank Capra discussing his Why We Fight series at the War College, 1941. (Bottom) A scene from Battle of Russia, one of the films in the Why We Fight series.

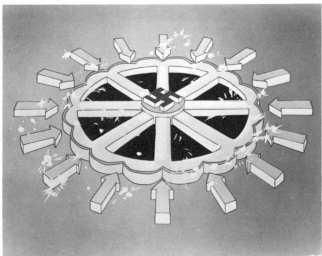

trian Anschluss to the invasion of Poland. This was followed by *Divide and Conquer* (1943) about the German invasion of Scandinavia, the Low Countries, and France. *The Battle of Britain* (1943) showed the gallant defense of England by the Royal Air Force. With the remaining films, *The Battle of Russia* (1943), *The Battle of China* (1944) and *War Comes to America* (1944), the American soldier was given a complete picture of the origins of the war and its progress. In Britain the entire series was shown to the public by order of Churchill himself.

Because of the opposition from Congress and Hollywood, few official propaganda films were made for domestic consumption. For audiences abroad the United States government financed its own newsreel series, "United Newsreels," which was released in sixteen languages for viewing in friendly and neutral countries. The government also produced the bimonthly *Army-Navy Screen Magazine*. This newsreel kept the armed forces informed about current events at home and abroad. It also reminded them of the factory workers who produced the weapons they fought with. In the later stages of the war these films gave details of the concentration camps in occupied Europe and Nazi cruelty to their defeated enemies. The films were accompanied by a lively use of the vernacular, to appeal directly to the G.I. in his own language.

More than a year before the capitulation of Japan, the War Department commissioned the film *Two Down, One to Go* to explain to American troops in Europe that even when Germany and Italy were beaten, Japan still remained. This was to counter the men's natural longing to return home in June of 1945. The film told them instead that they would soon be transferred to the Pacific theater of war.

The main conclusion to be drawn from the use of propaganda in and by the United States during World War II is that propaganda cannot do much against an enemy who is fresh and confident. It is only when defeat sets in, that propaganda begins to work. This situation started to develop in Europe within a year of America's entering the war. At the root of it all lay the American industrial system. Mass production was, and is, its specialty. A single example suffices. In the autumn of 1942, the United States had only three aircaft carriers. A year later there were fifty in the American fleet; by the end of the war, over 100. This extraordinary achievement was matched by an increase in aircraft production which was no less remarkable. It was merely a question of letting the enemy know this, and of the fearful retribution which would increase in geometrical progression with every extra day he resisted. This the Americans did primarily by leaflets, using their immense air fleets. Italian morale was broken, German confidence weakened, French resistance stimulated, and finally Japanese surrender obtained. Political propaganda, a device fundamentally distasteful to the American character, was most effectively employed by the neglected and often despised ad hoc organizations set up by President Roosevelt to help save the American people from themselves.

Isolationist sheet music cover, 1940/
USA/Artist unknown.

*Bubble gum "War Cards" carried the following legends "To know
the HORRORS OF WAR is to want PEACE," 1938/USA/Artist unknown.*

DECEMBER 7, 1941

*This caricature, appearing several days after Pearl Harbor, probably
did little to arouse American ire, 1941/USA/Arthur Szyk.*

As the war progressed, America felt more confident
about defeating Japan, 1944/USA/Artist unknown.

Poster produced for factory workers by Texaco,
c. 1943/USA/Artist unknown.

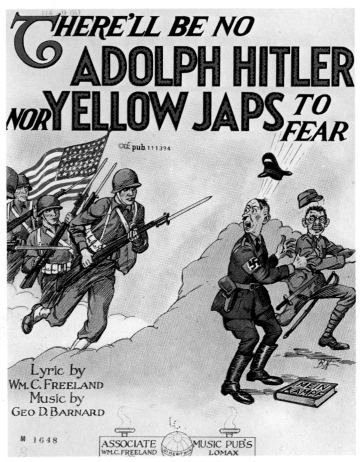

Patriotic songs, both serious and comic, boosted
American morale, no date/USA.

Even popular song themes promised Japan's defeat,
no date/USA/Artist unknown.

Even early in the war, Americans could laugh at Hitler, 1942/USA/Walt Disney Studio.

Adolf Hitler—Napoleon Jr., an early magazine caricature, 1933/USA/W. Cotton.

Hitler as an aspiring world conqueror, 1942/ USA/Boris Artzybasheff.

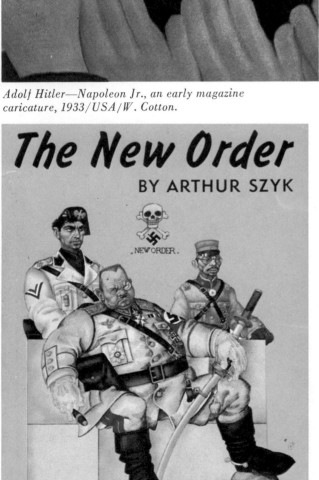

Cover for a book of anti-Axis drawings, 1941/ USA/Arthur Szyk.

Szyk's mordant caricatures sometimes appeared on Collier's *covers, 1942/USA/Arthur Szyk.*

Even Captain Freedom joined the fight against the Axis, c. 1943/USA/Schomberg.

Songs mocking the Nazis were popular with the public, no date/USA/Artist unknown.

Caricature showing Mussolini subservient to Germany and Japan, 1942/USA/Arthur Szyk.

*This aristocratic officer seems a far cry from the crudeness of most
Nazi leaders, 1942/USA/Karl Koehler and Victor Ancona.*

*The emotional appeal of the threatened mother and child
made this poster a success, 1942/Canada/G. K. Odell.*

A grim picture of Axis occupation to spur the American fighting spirit, 1942/USA/Ben Shahn.

*Again, c. 1943/USA/
Thomas Hart Benton.*

*The hooded figure and ticker-tape text made
this poster effective, 1942/USA/Ben Shahn.*

Connecting loose talk with a sunken ship,
1942/USA/Henry Koerner.

A more abstract statement of the careless talk
theme, 1943/USA/Steven Dohanos.

This poster was well designed but too sophisticated
to have much influence, c. 1943/USA/Steven Dohanos.

A simple image shows the results of careless
talk, c. 1943/USA/John Atherton.

Flagg's avuncular Uncle Sam got tough as victories
mounted, 1944/USA/James Montgomery Flagg.

This poster played on the theme that danger was also
close to home, 1942/USA/Artist unknown.

A realistic rendering of the American soldier
in combat, 1942/USA/Norman Rockwell.

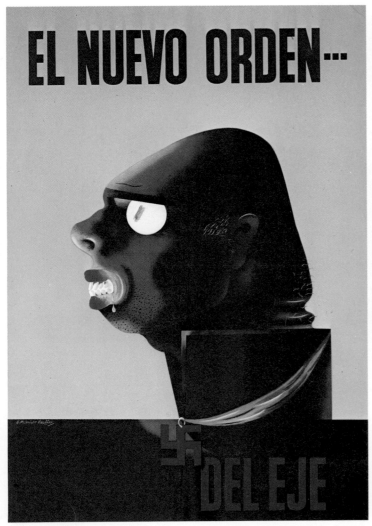

The New Order of the Axis (Office of Inter-American Affairs),
c. 1944/USA/E. McKnight Kauffer.

Hands Off the Americas (Office of Inter-American Affairs),
1942/USA/John Gaydos.

As One Man (Office of Inter-American Affairs),
c. 1942/USA/Arias Bernal.

Though strong graphically, this poster's message
and intent were unclear to factory workers,
1942/USA/Glenn Grohe.

When you ride ALONE you ride with Hitler!

Join a Car-Sharing Club TODAY!

Civilians were strongly exhorted to share resources, 1942/USA/Weimer Pursell.

STOP HIM

AND THE JOB'S DONE

The oversized Japanese soldier is intended to threaten the viewer, 1942/USA/Artist unknown.

STOP

STOP STEALING TOOLS! THAT CREW WILL NEED THEM IN COMBAT

A frank admittance that factory thefts occurred, even in wartime, 1944/USA/Artist unknown.

Stop this monster that stops at nothing... PRODUCE to the limit!

This is YOUR war!

A plea for more production to fend off the Axis brute, 1943/USA/Bert Yates.

(Top) Win the War issue, 1942/USA/Artist unknown. (Bottom) Issued to commemorate the battle of Iwo Jima, 1945/USA/Artist unknown.